GLAMKNITS

GLAMKNITS

25+ DESIGNS FOR LUXE YARNS

stefanie japel

NORTH LIGHT BOOKS
Cincinnati, Ohio
www.mycraftivity.com

Published by North Light Books, an imprint of F+W Publications, Inc., 4700 East Galbraith Road, Cincinnati, Ohio 45236. (800) 289-0963. First edition.

12 11 10 09 08   5 4 3 2 1

Distributed in Canada by Fraser Direct
100 Armstrong Avenue
Georgetown, ON, Canada L7G 5S4
Tel: (905) 877-4411

Distributed in the U.K. and Europe by David & Charles
Brunel House, Newton Abbot, Devon, TQ12 4PU, England
Tel: (+44) 1626 323200, Fax: (+44) 1626 323319
E-mail: postmaster@davidandcharles.co.uk

Distributed in Australia by Capricorn Link
P.O. Box 704, S. Windsor, NSW 2756 Australia
Tel: (02) 4577-3555

Library of Congress Cataloging-in-Publication Data

Japel, Stefanie.
  Glam knits : 25 designs for luxe yarns / by Stefanie Japel.
       p. cm.
  Includes index.
  ISBN-13: 978-1-60061-035-6
  1. Knitting--Patterns. I. Title.
  TT825.J387 2008
  746.43'2041--dc22
                                    2008017252

EDITOR: Jessica Gordon
ART DIRECTOR / DESIGNER: Karla Baker
ART DIRECTORS / PHOTOGRAPHY: Marissa Bowers, Karla Baker
PHOTOGRAPHER: Adam Leigh-Manuell, Alias Imaging LLC
STYLIST: Monica Skrzelowski
MAKE-UP ARTIST: Cass Brake
PRODUCTION COORDINATOR: Greg Nock
TECHNICAL EDITOR: Sue McCain

METRIC CONVERSION CHART

TO CONVERT	TO	MULTIPLY BY
Inches	Centimeters	2.54
Centimeters	Inches	0.4
Feet	Centimeters	30.5
Centimeters	Feet	0.03
Yards	Meters	0.9
Meters	Yards	1.1
Sq. Inches	Sq. Centimeters	6.45
Sq. Centimeters	Sq. Inches	0.16
Sq. Feet	Sq. Meters	0.09
Sq. Meters	Sq. Feet	10.8
Sq. Yards	Sq. Meters	0.8
Sq. Meters	Sq. Yards	1.2
Pounds	Kilograms	0.45
Kilograms	Pounds	2.2
Ounces	Grams	28.3
Grams	Ounces	0.035

F·W PUBLICATIONS, INC.

www.fwpublications.com

THIS BOOK IS DEDICATED TO MY DAUGHTER, MAZIE.

ACKNOWLEDGMENTS

Thank you to Leah Bear, Donna Warnell and Cathi Arfin for helping with the knitting for this book. I would like to thank my editor, Jessica Gordon, and my technical editor, Sue McCain, for their hard work. I also thank the kind folks at F+W Publications for their flexibility during the production of this book. And a big thank you to my mom, Linda, without whose babysitting help I would still be knitting the garments!

CONTENTS

INTRODUCTION:
WHAT MAKES A KNIT GLAM?

What makes a knit glam? It can be as complicated as intricate lacework or as simple as working a relaxing stitch pattern in an elegant yarn. Glamour is an almost indescribable quality that varies widely from person to person. However you define glam, there's something here to fit your style.

I've designed the garments in this book in many different styles of glam. Some garments are show-stopping centerpieces worked in all-over lace. Other pieces are worked in quieter stitches, such as Stockinette and seed stitch, offering a more under-stated take on glamour. My definition of glamour changes from day to day. Sometimes I need a small touch such as a purse or a scarf, and other days I want a fabulous coat or lace dress. With that in mind, I've included both small and large projects. Some of the smaller pieces in the book can be knit in an afternoon, while others are what I think of as Big Projects.

Regardless of what makes you feel glam, there's no knitting glam without great yarn. The yarns in this book vary in fiber content, gauge and cost, but they all have a distinctly fancy air about them. Some are spun with gold thread, while others are pure cushy cashmere or gleaming silk. While I have chosen

these yarns because to me they're truly gorgeous and very glam, it's completely possible to substitute them for yarns you may already have on hand. See the section on Working with Luxe Yarns (page 12) to read about the special qualities luxe yarns lend to knitted fabric, including luscious drape, subtle sparkle, extraordinary softness or an alluring halo.

Once you've chosen your yarn, make sure you're knitting a garment that fits you perfecly. After all, you can't be glam without a great fit. That's why every pattern in this book is sized from extra small through extra large. See the Fitting Your Knits section on page 14 to make sure you know how to choose the size that fits you best.

From daytime sophistication to all-out evening style, you'll find the perfect expression of your glam inside *Glam Knits*.

SKILL LEVEL GUIDE

Each pattern in the book is rated by skill level. Patterns rated as Supereasy are the simplest and most basic. If you're a newer knitter, you might want to start with those patterns. More intermediate-level patterns are rated as Medium, and they require a few more advanced skills. The Challenge-rated patterns are the most difficult and require a bit more complicated knitting operations. Don't let the skill-level rating stop you from knitting a pattern, but do be aware of what you need to know before you start. There's nothing worse than a knitting roadblock that stalls your project.

SUPEREASY

You must know how to cast on and off, knit and purl, do simple increases and decreases, pick up stitches and that's about it.

MEDIUM

You must know how to do the Supereasy stuff, be willing to do bust and waist shaping, knit simple cables and basic lace, and work buttonholes.

CHALLENGE

You must know how to do the Supereasy and Medium stuff and be willing to do more challenging techniques, such as applied I-cord, more intricate stitch work and more complex shaping.

WORKING WITH LUXE YARNS

Knitting a glam piece requires starting with glam yarn. All the patterns in this book call for luxurious yarns that really add to the glamorous quality of each piece. Whether they have extreme softness, extraordinary drape or even the sparkle of crystals or sequins, these luscious yarns are hard to resist. Following is a brief overview of the main yarns used in this book. Of course, feel free to make substitutions—just make sure to knit a gauge swatch to see if the yarn you choose creates the same effect as the one pictured.

ANGORA

Angora comes from the Angora rabbit, and it's the least expensive and most readily available luxury yarn. The mention of angora sweaters brings to mind images of 1940s and 1950s "Sweater Girls" pinup art. In this book, I've updated the angora cardigan (page 78) to a more free-fitting shape, but I've kept it sexy by knitting it in a delicate lace stitch. Angora gets a bad rap for fuzziness, but when spun correctly, it's a luxurious choice that's incredibly warm and soft.

CASHMERE

Cashmere comes from the soft, downy undercoat of the cashmere goat. The lightweight fiber is exquisitely soft, so it's perfect for any garment worn directly against your skin. It also has a lovely drape and sheen. Its wonderful insulating properties mean it adds warmth without increasing bulk. It makes a good choice for an airy cardigan that just floats around the body (see page 52). Of course, cashmere is one of the most expensive fibers money can buy, so most of us can't knit all of our projects using it. Cashmere is definitely one of those yarns for only the most special garments. Look for less expensive blends where cashmere is combined with merino, silk or baby alpaca.

MERINO

While merino simply denotes wool spun from the fleece of a specific breed of sheep, when using this yarn you can definitely tell you've upgraded. Merino is soft and cushy and holds its shape well. It's finer and softer than other varieties of wool, so it doesn't itch the skin. When worked single-ply (see the *Puff-Sleeved Hoodie*, page 104), merino is plush and has a shape-shifting quality—working with single-ply merino is like painting with watercolors. When processed in multiple plies (see the *Textured Circle Shrug*, page 82), it remains soft while simultaneously offering remarkable stitch definition.

MOHAIR

Mohair comes from Angora goats, and it has many of the same wonderful qualities as wool, plus it's warmer and stronger. Mohair sometimes gets a bad reputation for being stiff or prickly, but the mohair I've chosen is run along by a strand of pure silk and is the epitome of softness. In the *Deep U-Neck Tunic Dress* (page 66), I've chosen to let the yarn speak for itself—no lace or stitch patterns to distract you from the delicate mohair halo.

SILK

Silk is the fiber produced by silkworms as they spin their cocoons. When used as the sole fiber in any yarn, silk has a remarkable sheen that really belies its durability. While less expensive than cashmere, silk is still what I consider a special-occasion yarn. See the *Silk Skirt* (page 58) and the *Silk Cami* (page 18) to see just how luxurious silk can be. Silk does have a tendency to pill if not knit to a firm-enough gauge, and if you don't knit tightly enough, you may also find that your finished garment grows in length over time. As long as you maintain the proper tension, though, your silk garments will wear well and may turn out to be wardrobe staples!

EACH COLUMN TOP TO BOTTOM, FROM LEFT:
Tilli Tomas silk and silk-blend yarns; angora and angora-blend yarns; Southwest Trading Company's Vegas (wool/soysilk/metallic thread blend), mohair, cashmere; Vegas, baby alpaca

FITTING YOUR KNITS

One of the great things about knitting your own garments is that you can knit them so they fit you perfectly. That may mean making slight adjustments to the patterns to ensure they fit your body. Each of the patterns in this book is given for a wide range of sizes, from extra small to extra large. Determine which size to knit by choosing the bust size closest to yours. Then you can adjust the rest of the pattern accordingly, as necessary. To choose the correct size, you first need to know how to take your measurements. Following is a brief guide.

SHOULDER TO SHOULDER

This measurement is taken across the top of the shoulders, from one to the other at the widest point.

BUST

This measurement is taken at the fullest part of the bust by wrapping the measuring tape all the way around from front and center, around the back and to the front again. This measurement is given in inches (or centimeters) and corresponds to the size of garment you will make. Some texts give this measurement for the entire circumference (34" [86cm], for example), while others give this as the "lying flat" measurement (in the case above, it would be 17" [43cm]).

WAIST

To take your waist measurement, measure around the smallest circumference of your torso above the hips. Even though our pants don't sit here anymore, this is your "natural waist."

HIPS

For some of the garments in this book, you will want to take a hip measurement. Here you measure the widest part of your hips, including your backside.

ARMS

It is also important to know the length of your arms from *both* the shoulder to the wrist and from the underarm to the wrist. Many an hour can be saved if you take this measurement before you cast off that sleeve!

USING YOUR MEASUREMENTS TO ADJUST PATTERNS

Use your measurements to adjust patterns for the optimal fit.

After taking your measurements, choose the pattern that has the closest bust measurement to yours. Compare your measurements to those on the schematic to see if you need to make adjustments to waist measurement or to body or sleeve length. As you work the pattern, whether it's knit in the round or flat, you can work a few decreases to nip a pattern in at the waist, or you can add (or subtract) a few rows in order to alter the length if necessary. Be sure to add or subtract rows either before or after any shaping in the pattern so extra (or fewer) rows don't interfere with the "line" of the design.

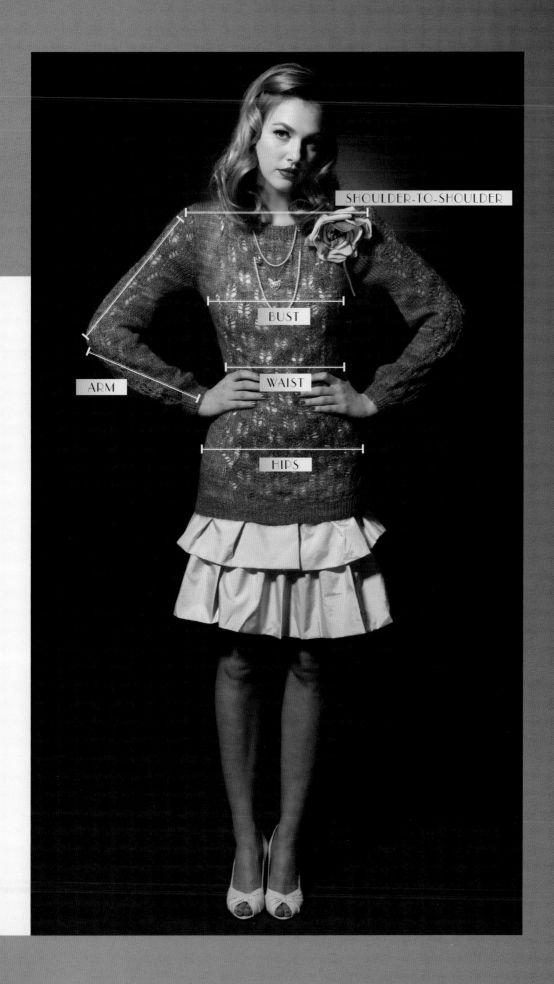

SHOULDER-TO-SHOULDER

BUST

ARM

WAIST

HIPS

SHOW IT OFF
CAMISOLES, TUNICS AND SWEATERS

The garments in this chapter are those key pieces that can really focus an outfit. From the balloon shaping of the *Bamboo Tunic* (see page 22) to the slim fit of the *Fitted Deep-Ribbed Cardigan* (see page 46), there's a style here for every occasion. One of my favorite current fashion trends is the tunic. I love its slimming lines and longer length. Tunics look great with wide-leg trousers, skinny jeans, leggings or over flirty skirts. Whatever your style, you can build an eye-catching look around any of these great tops.

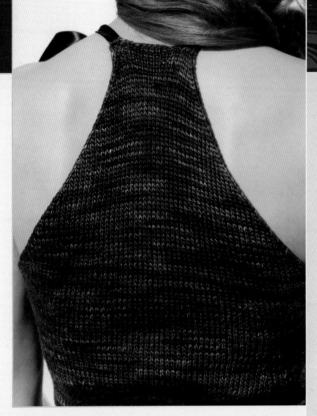

SILK CAMI

Here I combine two of my favorite silk yarns, Pure and Simple and Disco Lights, both by Tilli Tomas. I love the sheen of the Pure and Simple, and Disco Lights has just enough sparkle to make me really happy! The cami is knit from the hemline to the neckline, starting in lace and ending in a silk ribbon. If you don't like the look of the ribbon, simply knit both shoulder straps to match and close the second one with a snap, hook or pretty button. (This cami coordinates with the *Silk Skirt* on page 58.)

FINISHED MEASUREMENTS

TO FIT BUST: 32 (36, 40, 44, 48, 52)" (81 [91, 102, 112, 122, 132]cm)

YARN

2 (2, 3, 3, 3, 4) hanks (260 yds [234m] ea) Tilli Tomas Pure and Simple (100% spun silk)

COLOR GLAMPYRE (MC)

2 (2, 2, 2, 3, 3) hanks (225 yds [203m] ea) Tilli Tomas Disco Lights (spun silk/petite sequins blend)

COLOR SAPPHIRE (CC)

NEEDLES

size US 6 (4mm) 24", 29", 32" or 40" (60cm, 74cm, 80cm or 102cm) circular needle

2 size US 6 (4mm) double-pointed needles (dpn)

If necessary, change needle size to obtain correct gauge.

NOTIONS

stitch markers

scrap yarn

darning needle

sewing needle and thread

2 yds (2m) 1½" (4cm) wide satin ribbon

GAUGE

24 sts and 30 rows = 4" (10cm) in St st

NOTES

YO (YARN OVER): Wrap the working yarn around the needle clockwise and knit the next st as usual. This operation creates an eyelet hole in the knitting and inc 1 st.

SK2P (SLIP 1, KNIT 2 TOGETHER, PASS SLIPPED STITCH OVER): Dec 2 sts by knitting 2 sts tog and passing the slipped st over the st rem after the 2 sts were knit tog.

PM (PLACE MARKER): Slip a premade marker or a loosely knotted piece of scrap yarn in a contrasting color onto the right-hand needle after the stitch just knit to mark a spot in the knitting to refer to on future rows. When you come to a marker, simply slip it from the right-hand needle to the left-hand needle.

SSK (SLIP, SLIP, KNIT): Dec 1 st by slipping 2 sts knitwise one at a time, inserting the tip of the left needle into both sts and knitting the 2 sts tog.

K2TOG (KNIT 2 TOGETHER): Dec 1 st by knitting 2 sts tog.

SSSK (SLIP, SLIP, SLIP, KNIT): Dec 2 sts by slipping 3 sts knitwise one at a time, inserting the tip of the left needle into all 3 sts and knitting the sts tog.

K3TOG (KNIT 3 TOGETHER): Dec 2 sts by knitting 3 sts tog.

M1 (MAKE 1): Inc 1 st by picking up the bar between the next st and the st just knit and knitting into it.

FISHTAIL LACE

Work fishtail lace over a multiple of 8 sts.

RND 1 (RS): *K1, yo, k2, SK2P, k2; rep from * around.

RNDS 2 AND 4: Knit.

RND 3: *K2, yo, k1, SK2P, k1, yo, k1; rep from * around.

RND 5: *K3, yo, SK2P, yo, k2; rep from * around.

RND 6: Knit.

Rep Rnds 1–6.

BODY

With CC, cast on 200 (224, 248, 272, 296, 320) sts. Join for working in the rnd, pm. Work in fishtail lace for 36 rnds (6 vertical patt rep).

NEXT RND: Work in St st until piece measures 11½ (12, 12½, 13, 13½, 14)" (29 [30, 32, 33, 34, 36]cm) from beg.

SHAPE BODY

NEXT RND: K25 (28, 31, 34, 37, 40), pm, [k50 (56, 62, 68, 74, 80), pm] 3 times, k25 (28, 31, 34, 37, 40).

Work 1 rnd even.

DEC RND: [Knit to 3 sts before marker, SSK, k2, k2tog] 4 times, knit to end—192 (216, 240, 264, 288, 312) sts rem.

Work 3 rnds even.

Rep last 4 rnds 3 times more—168 (192, 216, 240, 264, 288) sts rem.

Work 2 rnds even.

SEPARATE BACK AND FRONT

Place last 84 (96, 108, 120, 132, 144) sts worked on scrap yarn for front to be worked later.

BACK

DEC ROW 1 (RS): K2, SSK, knit to last 4 sts, k2tog, k2—82 (94, 106, 118, 130, 142) sts rem.

Work 1 row even.

Rep last 2 rows 33 (29, 27, 23, 19, 13) times more—16 (36, 52, 72, 92, 116) sts rem.

SIZES 36 (40, 44, 48, 52)

DEC ROW 2 (RS): K2, SSSK, knit to last 5 sts, k3tog, k2—32 (48, 68, 88, 112) sts rem.

Work 1 row even.

Rep last 2 rows 4 (7, 12, 16, 22) times more—16 (20, 20, 24, 24) sts rem.

ALL SIZES

NEXT ROW (RS): K5 (5, 6, 6, 7, 7) and place these sts on scrap yarn to be worked later, bind off rem 11 (11, 14, 14, 17, 17) sts.

FRONT

Transfer 84 (96, 108, 120, 132, 144) held sts of front to needle.

DEC ROW 1 (RS): K2, SSK, knit to last 4 sts, k2tog, k2—82 (94, 106, 118, 130, 142) sts rem.

Work 1 row even.

INC ROW (RS): K2, SSK, k10 (10, 10, 11, 11, 12), [M1, k5] 11 times, M1, knit to last 4 sts, k2tog, k2—92 (104, 116, 128, 140, 152) sts.

Work 1 row even.

Work Dec Row once more—90 (102, 114, 126, 138, 150) sts rem.

Work 1 row even.

Rep last 2 rows 20 (20, 20, 18, 16, 10) times more—50 (62, 74, 90, 106, 130) sts rem.

SIZES 36 (40, 44, 48, 52)

DEC ROW 2 (RS): K2, SSSK, knit to last 5 sts, k3tog, k2—58 (70, 86, 102, 126) sts rem.

Work 1 row even.

Rep last 2 rows 2 (4, 8, 11, 17) times more—50 (54, 54, 58, 58) sts rem.

ALL SIZES

NEXT ROW (RS): K2, SSK, k11 (11, 12, 12, 13, 13), k2tog, k2, join a second ball of yarn and bind off center 20 (20, 22, 22, 24, 24) sts (1 st on right-hand needle), k1, SSK, k11 (11, 12, 12, 13, 13), k2tog, k2—13 (13, 14, 14, 15, 15) sts rem each side.

Working both sides at same time, work 1 row even.

NEXT ROW (RS): Each side: k2, SSK, knit to last 4 sts on side, k2tog, k2—11 (11, 12, 12, 13, 13) sts rem each side.

Work 1 row even.

Rep last 2 rows 2 (2, 3, 3, 3, 3) times more—7 (7, 6, 6, 7, 7) sts rem each side.

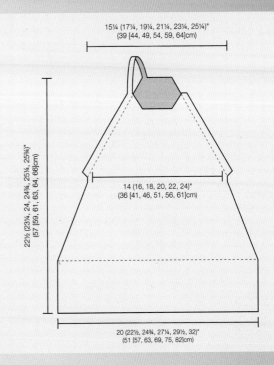

15¼ (17¼, 19¼, 21¼, 23¼, 25¼)"
(39 [44, 49, 54, 59, 64]cm)

22½ (23¾, 24, 24¾, 25¼, 25¾)"
(57 [59, 61, 63, 64, 66]cm)

14 (16, 18, 20, 22, 24)"
(36 [41, 46, 51, 56, 61]cm)

20 (22½, 24¾, 27¼, 29½, 32)"
(51 [57, 63, 69, 75, 82]cm)

SIZE 32

NEXT ROW (RS): Each side: k2, SSK, k3—6 sts rem each side.

Work 1 row even.

NEXT ROW (RS): Each side: k2, SSK, k2—5 sts rem each side.

Work 1 row even.

ALL SIZES

NEXT ROW (RS): Left side: bind off; Right side: work 5 (5, 6, 6, 7, 7)-st I-cord for 5 (5, 6, 6, 7, 7)" (13 [13, 15, 15, 18, 18]cm).

Using Kitchener st (see page 140 in the Special Techniques Glossary), graft sts to back sts on holder.

Note: Try on camisole before grafting and adjust length of I-cord if necessary to reach back sts.

FINISHING

Weave in ends.

Cut ribbon into 2 equal lengths. Fold 1 end of each length in half widthwise. Attach 1 end of 1 ribbon at the left front and 1 ribbon at the left back using a sewing needle and thread.

BAMBOO TUNIC

Knit from the top down in shimmery Berroco Bonsai, this tunic is simple but still shines. The closures at the neck are tiny gold buckles (I found them in the hobby section of my local fabric and craft store). The tunic is oversized and shaped with a nod to the Balloon Tunic of the 1980s, with an updated shape. The drawstring at the hips ensures *your* shape remains defined. Pair this tunic with a pair of sparkly leggings for a night out or with jeans and boots for daytime.

FINISHED MEASUREMENTS

TO FIT BUST: 32–34 (36–38, 40–42, 44–46, 48–50)" (81–86 [91–97, 102–107, 112–117, 122–127]cm)

ACTUAL BUST: 38¾ (42¾, 46¾, 50¾, 54¾)" (98 [109, 119, 129, 139]cm)

YARN

13 (14, 16, 18, 19) hanks (77 yds [69m] ea) Berroco Bonsai (bamboo/nylon blend)

COLOR 4141 JAPANESE MAPLE

NEEDLES

size US 7 (4.5mm) 29", 32" or 40" (74cm, 80cm or 102cm) circular needle

If necessary, change needle size to obtain correct gauge.

NOTIONS

stitch markers

darning needle

sewing needle and thread

2 gold-tone mini buckles (found at hobby store)

2 (2, 2¼, 2½, 2¾) yds (1.75 [1.75, 2, 2.25, 2.5]m) gold cord

GAUGE

20 sts and 27 rows = 4" (10cm) in St st

NOTES

PM (PLACE MARKER): Slip a premade marker or a loosely knotted piece of scrap yarn in a contrasting color onto the right-hand needle after the stitch just knit to mark a spot in the knitting to refer to on future rows. When you come to a marker, simply slip it from the right-hand needle to the left-hand needle.

[ ] (REPEAT OPERATION): Rep the bracketed operation the number of times indicated.

KFB (KNIT 1 FRONT AND BACK): Inc 1 st by knitting into the front and back of the next st.

SL MARKER OR SL ST(S) (SLIP MARKER OR SLIP STITCH[ES]): Slip a st or sts purlwise from the left needle to the right needle. When slipping a marker, knit the sts before and after it as usual.

K2TOG (KNIT 2 TOGETHER): Dec 1 st by knitting 2 sts tog.

YO (YARN OVER): Wrap the working yarn around the needle clockwise and knit the next st as usual. This operation creates an eyelet hole in the knitting and inc 1 st.

M1 (MAKE 1): Inc 1 st by picking up the bar between the next st and the st just knit and knitting into it.

YOKE

Cast on 152 (156, 160, 164, 168) sts. Do not join. Work 8 rows in garter st.

NEXT ROW (RS): K8 (edge sts, keep in garter st), work in St st to last 8 sts, k8 (edge sts, keep in garter st).

Work 1 row even.

NEXT ROW: Keeping edge sts in garter st, work 25 (26, 25, 26, 27) sts for right front, pm, 26 (26, 30, 30, 30) sts for sleeve, pm, 50 (52, 50, 52, 54) sts for back, pm, 26 (26, 30, 30, 30) sts for sleeve, pm, then 25 (26, 25, 26, 27) sts for left front.

Work 1 row even.

RAGLAN INC ROW: [Work to 1 st before marker, KFB, sl marker, KFB] 4 times, work to end—160 (164, 168, 172, 176) sts.

Rep last 2 rows 7 (7, 9, 9, 9) times—216 (220, 240, 244, 248) sts. Work 1 row even.

NEXT ROW: Work to 1 st before marker, KFB, sl marker, bind off 42 (42, 50, 50, 50) sleeve sts, sl marker, work across 66 (68, 70, 72, 74) back sts, sl marker, bind off 42 (42, 50, 50, 50) sleeve sts, sl marker, KFB, work to end—134 (138, 142, 146, 150) sts rem.

NEXT ROW: [Work to bound-off sts, sl 1 marker, cast on 10 (18, 26, 34, 42) sts using Backward-Loop method (see the Special Techniques Glossary, page 138), sl marker] twice, work to end—154 (174, 194, 214, 234) sts.

NEXT ROW: [Work to 1 st before marker, KFB, sl marker, KFB] 4 times, work to end—162 (182, 202, 222, 242) sts.

NEXT ROW: [Work to marker, sl marker, knit to next marker] twice, work to end.

Rep last 2 rows 4 times—194 (214, 234, 254, 274) sts. Do not turn.

BODY

Join for working in the rnd.

Knit to 5 (9, 13, 17, 21) sts after first marker, removing marker. Pm for beg of rnd.

Work in St st, removing all markers on first rnd except beg of rnd marker, and omitting garter sts at center front, until piece measures 16½ (17, 17½, 18, 18½)" (42 [43, 44, 46, 47]cm) from underarm.

NEXT RND: K2tog, k12 (8, 12, 10, 12), *k2tog, k10 (10, 9, 9, 11); rep from * around—178 (196, 213, 231, 253) sts rem.

Work 4 rnds in garter st, beg with a purl rnd.

EYELET RND: K8 (12, 11, 9, 9), yo, k2tog, *k10 (11, 8, 9, 9), yo, k2tog; rep from * around.

Work 5 rnds in garter st, beg with a knit rnd.

NEXT RND: K8 (6, 8, 6, 8), M1, *k5, M1; rep from * around—213 (235, 255, 277, 303) sts.

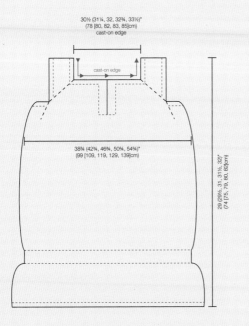

30½ (31¼, 32, 32¾, 33½)"
(78 [80, 82, 83, 85]cm)
cast-on edge

cast-on edge

38¾ (42¾, 46¾, 50¾, 54¾)"
(99 [109, 119, 129, 139]cm)

29 (29¾, 31, 31½, 32)"
(74 [75, 79, 80, 82]cm)

Work in St st until piece measures 22½ (23, 23½, 24, 24½)" [57 (58, 60, 61, 62)cm] from underarm.

Work 7 rnds in garter st, beg with a purl rnd.

Bind off.

FINISHING

CLOSURES (MAKE 2)

Cast on 20 sts. Work 2 rows in garter st. Bind off.

Sew the first closure to the left edge of the front placket, just below the garter st yoke edge, and sew the second closure ¼" (6mm) below the first. Sew buckles to the right edge of the front placket, opposite the closures.

Weave in ends. Thread gold cord through eyelets.

ZIGZAG LACE
WRAPAROUND

Knit from an alpaca blend, this lace tunic transitions easily from day to night. Side-to-side knitting orients the lace pattern vertically, which gives it a long, lean silhouette. Wear it over a stretchy tank dress, skinny trousers or just a silk slip, if you dare!

FINISHED MEASUREMENTS

TO FIT BUST: 34–40 (42–48, 50–56)" (86–102 [107–122, 127–142]cm)

ACTUAL BUST: 41½ (50, 58½)" (105 [127, 149]cm)

NOTE: *This design has a considerable amount of ease—between 6" (15cm) and 7" (18cm). When knitting the "to fit bust" size (the size corresponding to your actual measurement), you'll end up with a finished garment with "actual bust" sizes as listed.*

YARN

5 (7, 8) hanks (140 yds [126m] ea) Blue Sky Alpacas Alpaca Silk (alpaca/silk blend)
  COLOR 123 RUBY

NEEDLES

size US 9 (5.5mm) straight needles

size US 4 (3.5mm) 29" (74cm) circular needle

If necessary, change needle size to obtain correct gauge.

NOTIONS

stitch markers

scrap yarn

darning needle

GAUGE

14½ sts and 23 rows = 4" (10cm) in cockleshell lace (see page 28), using larger needle

NOTE: *Because this yarn is very drapey, you may want to hang your swatch for a few days before measuring the gauge. This will give the swatch time to "grow" so you can take a more accurate gauge measurement.*

NOTES

K3TOG (KNIT 3 TOGETHER): Dec 2 sts by knitting 3 sts tog.

YO (YARN OVER): Wrap the working yarn around the needle clockwise and knit the next st as usual. This operation creates an eyelet hole in the knitting and inc 1 st.

PM (PLACE MARKER): Slip a premade marker or a loosely knotted piece of scrap yarn in a contrasting color onto the right-hand needle after the stitch just knit to mark a spot in the knitting to refer to on future rows. When you come to a marker, simply slip it from the right-hand needle to the left-hand needle.

COCKLESHELL LACE

Work cockleshell lace over a multiple of 14 sts + 1.

ROW 1 AND ALL WS ROWS (WS): Knit.

ROW 2: K1, *k1, yo, k5, k3tog, k5, yo, k1; rep from * to end.

ROW 4: K1, *k2, yo, k4, k3tog, k4, yo, k2; rep from * to end.

ROW 6: K1, *k3, yo, k3, k3tog, k3, yo, k3; rep from * to end.

ROW 8: K1, *k4, yo, k2, k3tog, k2, yo, k4; rep from * to end.

ROW 10: K1, *k5, yo, k1, k3tog, k1, yo, k5; rep from * to end.

ROW 12: K1, *k6, yo, k3tog, yo, k6; rep from * to end.

Rep Rows 1–12.

BACK (MAKE 2)

With larger needle, cast on 85 sts. Work 60 (72, 84) rows [5 (6, 7) vertical rep] in cockleshell lace. Place sts on scrap yarn to be worked later. When second piece has been completed, graft pieces together using Kitchener st (see page 140 in the Special Techniques Glossary).

RIGHT FRONT

With larger needle, cast on 85 sts. Work 36 (48, 48) rows (3 [4, 4] vertical rep) in cockleshell lace.

SHAPE RIGHT FRONT

SIZES 41½ (50)

NEXT ROW (WS): Work 48 (60) more rows (4 [5] vertical rep) in cockleshell lace, and at the same time, BO 3 sts at beg of each RS row 22 (10) times, then bind off 2 sts at beg of each RS row 2 (20) times—15 sts rem.

Bind off.

SIZE 58½

NEXT ROW (WS): Work 84 more rows (7 vertical rep) in cockleshell lace, and at the same time, bind off 2 sts at beg of each RS row 28 times, then dec 1 st at beg of each RS row 14 times—15 sts rem.

Bind off.

LEFT FRONT

With larger needle, cast on 85 sts. Work 36 (48, 48) rows (3 [4, 4] vertical rep) in cockleshell lace. Work 1 more row in cockleshell lace.

SHAPE LEFT FRONT

SIZES 41½ (50)

NEXT ROW (RS): Work 47 (59) more rows (4 [5] vertical rep) in cockleshell lace, and at the same time, bind off 3 sts at beg of each RS row 22 (10) times, then bind off 2 sts at beg of each WS row 2 (20) times—15 sts rem.

Bind off.

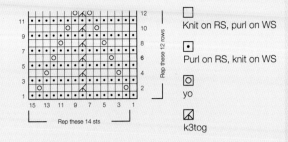

☐	Knit on RS, purl on WS
▪	Purl on RS, knit on WS
Ø	yo
☒	k3tog

SIZE 58½

NEXT ROW (RS): Work 83 more rows (7 vertical rep) in cockleshell lace, and at the same time, bind off 2 sts at beg of each WS row 28 times, then dec 1 st at beg of each RS row 14 times—15 sts rem.

Bind off.

FINISHING

Block all pieces. Seam shoulders.

Seam the sides, being careful to match the lace patt, and seaming the front edges tog into the side seams so that the fronts overlap, with the right front on top of the left front; the bound-off edge of the right front should be in front of the cast-on edge of the left front, and the bound-off edge of the left front should be behind the cast-on edge of the right front.

RIBBING

With circular needle, beg at left side seam, pick up and knit approx 3 sts for every 4 rows around bottom edge of body, picking up sts in both fronts together and ending with a multiple of 4 sts. Join for working in the rnd, pm. Work in k2, p2 rib for 4" (10cm). Bind off loosely in patt.

Weave in ends.

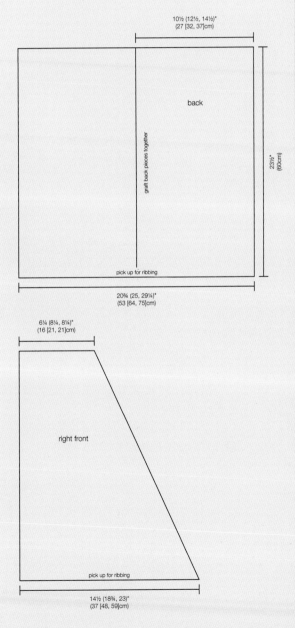

BOHO BLOUSE

A cape sleeve is created by extending the yoke of the sweater almost to the elbow, creating a flowy, flirty fabric with lots of movement. This top-down blouse is embellished with single cable twists on a Stockinette background, bordered by garter rows that encase eyelets for a peek of skin. To wear this top as an outer layer, make a size larger than you would normally make for your bust measurement. This top looks equally great with a peasant skirt or skinny jeans.

FINISHED MEASUREMENTS

BUST: 32 (36, 44½, 53½)" (81 [91, 113, 136]cm)

YARN

4 (5, 6, 7) hanks (120 yds [108m] ea) Lorna's Laces Swirl Chunky (merino/silk blend)
COLOR CHOCOLATE

NEEDLES

size US 10½ (6.5mm) 20", 32", 40" or 60" (51cm, 81cm, 102cm or 152cm) circular needle

If necessary, change needle size to obtain correct gauge.

NOTIONS

stitch marker
cable needle
darning needle

GAUGE

12 sts and 17 rows = 4" (10cm) in St st

NOTES

K2TOG (KNIT 2 TOGETHER): Dec 1 st by knitting 2 sts tog.

YO (YARN OVER): Wrap the working yarn around the needle clockwise, and knit the next st as usual. This operation creates an eyelet hole in the knitting and inc 1 st.

PM (PLACE MARKER): Slip a premade marker or a loosely knotted piece of scrap yarn in a contrasting color onto the right-hand needle after the stitch just knit to mark a spot in the knitting to refer to on future rows. When you come to a marker, simply slip it from the right-hand needle to the left-hand needle.

M1 (MAKE 1): Inc 1 st by picking up the bar between the next st and the st just knit and knitting into it.

C5F (CABLE 5 FRONT): Slip 3 sts to a cable needle, hold the sts to the front, k2, then k3 from the cable needle.

TRIM PATTERN

Work trim patt over a multiple of 2 sts.

RND 1: Purl.

RND 2: *K2tog, yo; rep from * around.

RND 3: Knit.

RND 4: Purl.

RNDS 5–6: Knit.

RNDS 7–10: Rep Rnds 1–4.

YOKE

Cast on 60 (74, 90, 104) sts, pm and join for working in the rnd, taking care not to twist sts. Work 10 rnds in trim patt, inc 0 (1, 0, 1) st on last rnd—60 (75, 90, 105) sts.

SHAPE YOKE

INC RND 1: *K3, M1; rep from * around—80 (100, 120, 140) sts.

Work 4 (8, 8, 8) rnds in St st.

BEGIN CABLE PATTERN

CABLE RND 1: *K15, C5F; rep from * around.

Work 1 rnd in St st.

INC RND 2: *K2, M1; rep from * around—120 (150, 180, 210) sts.

Work 2 rnds in St st.

CABLE RND 2: K5, *C5F, k25; rep from * to last 25 sts, C5F, k20.

Work 4 rnds in St st.

CABLE RND 3: K15, *C5F, k25; rep from * to last 15 sts, C5F, k10.

Work 1 rnd in St st.

INC RND 3: *K3, M1; rep from * around—160 (200, 240, 280) sts.

Work 2 rnds in St st.

CABLE RND 4: K30, *C5F, k35; rep from * to last 10 sts, C5F, k5.

Work 4 rnds in St st.

CABLE RND 5: K5, *C5F, k35; rep from * to last 35 sts, C5F, k30.

Work 4 rnds in St st.

CABLE RND 6: K20, *C5, k35; rep from * to last 20 sts, C5F, k15.

Work 4 (4, 7, 9) rnds in St st.

Work 10 rnds in trim patt.

SEPARATE SLEEVE CAPS FROM BODY

NEXT RND: Bind off next 32 (46, 53, 60) sts for first sleeve cap, k48 (54, 67, 80) sts, bind off next 32 (46, 53, 60) sts for second sleeve cap, knit to end—96 (108, 134, 160) sts rem.

Work even until piece measures 7 (7, 7½, 8)" (18 [18, 19, 20]cm) from underarm. Work 10 rnds in trim patt. Bind off.

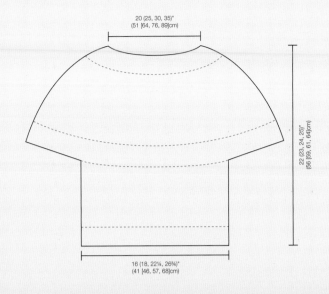

20 (25, 30, 35)"
(51 [64, 76, 89]cm)

22 (23, 24, 25)"
(56 [59, 61, 64]cm)

16 (18, 22¼, 26¾)"
(41 [46, 57, 68]cm)

BELL-SLEEVED
SCOOP-NECK TOP

Knit from fuzzy-soft Suri alpaca, this pullover is a perfect pick-me-up on a cloudy day. The yarn is so lightweight and soft you'll reach for this sweater on days when you just need to hear a whispered "I love you!" Wearing it is like a gentle kiss on the shoulder.

FINISHED MEASUREMENTS

BUST: 35 (39, 43½, 47½, 51, 55)" (89 [99, 110, 121, 130, 140]cm)

YARN

9 (10, 11, 13, 14, 15) hanks (142 yds [128m] ea) Blue Sky Alpacas Brushed Suri (baby Suri/merino/bamboo blend)
COLOR 907 PINK LEMONADE

NEEDLES

size US 7 (4.5mm) 29" (74cm) circular needle

size US 9 (5.5mm) 24", 32" or 40" (61cm, 81cm or 102cm) circular needle

size US 10½ (6.5mm) 32" (81cm) circular needle

5 size US 9 (5.5mm) double-pointed needles (dpn)

5 size US 10½ (6.5mm) double-pointed needles (dpn)

If necessary, change needle size to obtain correct gauge.

NOTIONS

stitch markers

scrap yarn

darning needle

GAUGE

16 sts and 26 rows = 4" (10cm) in St st using size US 9 needle

NOTES

K2TOG (KNIT 2 TOGETHER): Dec 1 st by knitting 2 sts tog.

YO (YARN OVER): Wrap the working yarn around the needle clockwise and knit the next st as usual. This operation creates an eyelet hole in the knitting and inc 1 st.

PM (PLACE MARKER): Slip a premade marker or a loosely knotted piece of scrap yarn in a contrasting color onto the right-hand needle after the stitch just knit to mark a spot in the knitting to refer to on future rows. When you come to a marker, simply slip it from the right-hand needle to the left-hand needle.

[ ] (REPEAT OPERATION): Rep the bracketed operation the number of times indicated.

SL MARKER OR SL ST(S) (SLIP MARKER OR SLIP STITCH[ES]): Slip a st or sts purlwise from the left needle to the right needle. When slipping a marker, knit the sts before and after it as usual.

KFB (KNIT 1 FRONT AND BACK): Inc 1 st by knitting into the front and back of the next st.

SSK (SLIP, SLIP, KNIT): Dec 1 st by slipping 2 sts knitwise one at a time, inserting the tip of the left needle into both sts and knitting the 2 sts tog.

M1 (MAKE 1): Inc 1 st by picking up the bar between the next st and the st just knit and knitting into it.

TRIM PATTERN

Work trim patt over a multiple of 2 sts.

RND 1: Purl.

RND 2: *K2tog, yo; rep from * around.

RND 3: Knit.

RND 4: Purl.

RNDS 5 AND 6: Knit.

RNDS 7–18: Rep Rnds 1–6.

RNDS 19–22: Rep Rnds 1–4.

RND 23: Knit.

RND 24: Purl.

RND 25: Knit.

NECK TRIM PATTERN

Work neck trim patt over a multiple of 2 sts.

RND 1: Purl.

RND 2: *K2tog, yo; rep from * around.

RND 3: Knit.

RND 4: Purl.

RND 5: Knit.

RNDS 6–8: Rep Rnds 1–3.

YOKE

With size US 9 (5.5mm) needle, cast on 58 (58, 60, 60, 62, 62) sts. Do not join.

RAGLAN SET-UP ROW (WS): P1, pm, p12 (12, 12, 10, 10, 8), pm, p32 (32, 34, 38, 40, 44), pm, p12 (12, 12, 10, 10, 8), pm, p1.

RAGLAN INC ROW 1 (RS): KFB, sl marker, KFB, [knit to 1 st before marker, KFB, sl marker, KFB] 3 times—66 (66, 68, 68, 70, 70) sts.

Work 1 row even.

RAGLAN INC ROW 2 (RS): [Knit to 1 st before marker, KFB, sl marker, KFB] 4 times, knit to end—74 (74, 76, 76, 78, 78) sts.

Work 1 row even.

Rep last 2 rows 10 (14, 15, 17, 20, 23) times more—154 (186, 196, 212, 238, 262) sts.

SHAPE FRONT NECK

NECK AND RAGLAN INC ROW 1 (RS): Cast on 2 sts, [knit to 1 st before marker, KFB, sl marker, KFB] 4 times, knit to end, cast on 2 sts—166 (198, 208, 224, 250, 274) sts.

Work 1 row even.

Rep last 2 rows 3 times more—202 (234, 244, 260, 286, 310) sts.

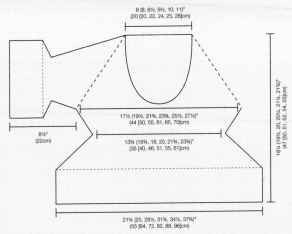

8 (8, 8½, 9½, 10, 11)"
(20 [20, 22, 24, 25, 28]cm)

18½ (19½, 20, 20½, 21½, 21¾)"
(47 [50, 51, 52, 54, 55]cm)

17½ (19½, 21¾, 23¾, 25½, 27½)"
(44 [50, 55, 61, 65, 70]cm)

13¾ (15¾, 18, 20, 21¾, 23¾)"
(35 [40, 46, 51, 55, 61]cm)

8½"
(22cm)

21¾ (25, 28½, 31¾, 34½, 37¾)"
(55 [64, 72, 82, 88, 96]cm)

NECK AND RAGLAN INC ROW 2 (RS): Cast on 4 sts, [knit to 1 st before marker, KFB, sl marker, KFB] 4 times, knit to end, cast on 4 sts—218 (250, 260, 276, 302, 326) sts.

Work 1 row even.

NECK AND RAGLAN INC ROW 3 (RS): Cast on 6 sts, [knit to 1 st before marker, KFB, sl marker, KFB] 4 times, knit to end—232 (264, 274, 290, 316, 340) sts.

Work 1 row even.

NEXT RND: Join for working in the rnd, pm, [knit to 1 st before marker, KFB, sl marker, KFB] 4 times, knit to end—240 (272, 282, 298, 324, 348) sts.

Work 1 rnd even.

BODY

SEPARATE SLEEVES FROM BODY

NEXT RND: Knit to marker, place next 50 (58, 60, 62, 68, 72) sts for first sleeve on scrap yarn to be worked later, cast on 0 (0, 3, 4, 4, 4) sts for underarm, pm for new beg of rnd, cast on 0 (0, 3, 4, 4, 4) sts, knit to next marker, place next 50 (58, 60, 62, 68, 72) sts for second sleeve on scrap yarn to be worked later, cast on 0 (0, 6, 8, 8, 8) sts for underarm, knit to new beg of rnd—140 (156, 174, 190, 204, 220) sts.

Work 4 rnds even.

SHAPE WAIST

WAIST SET-UP RND: K35 (39, 44, 49, 53, 58), pm, k52 (58, 65, 71, 77, 83), pm, k36 (40, 44, 48, 50, 54), pm, knit to end.

WAIST DEC RND: [Knit to 2 sts before marker, SSK, k2tog] 3 times, knit to end—134 (150, 168, 184, 198, 214) sts rem.

Work 1 rnd even.

Rep last 2 rnds 4 times more—110 (126, 144, 160, 174, 190) sts rem.

NEXT RND: Change to size US 10½ (6.5mm) circular needle.

Work 4 rnds even.

SIZES 35 (39, 51, 55)

INC RND: *K4, M1; rep from * to last 2 sts, knit 2, M1—138 (158, 218, 238) sts.

Work 1 rnd even, inc 0 (0, 0, 2) sts evenly around—138 (158, 218, 240) sts.

SIZES 43½ (47½)

INC RND: *K4, M1; rep from * around—180 (200) sts.

Work 1 rnd even.

ALL SIZES

NEXT RND: *K5, p1; rep from * to last 0 (2, 0, 2, 2, 0) sts, k0 (2, 0, 2, 2, 0).

Work 2 rnds even.

NEXT RND: *P1, k5; rep from * to last 0 (2, 0, 2, 2, 0) sts, k0 (2, 0, 2, 2, 0).

Work 2 rnds even.

NEXT RND: *K5, p1; rep from * to last 0 (2, 0, 2, 2, 0) sts, k0 (2, 0, 2, 2, 0).

Work 2 rnds even.

NEXT RND: Work 25 rnds in trim patt. Bind off purlwise.

SLEEVES

NEXT RND: Cast on 0 (0, 3, 4, 4, 4) sts, k50 (58, 60, 62, 68, 72) sts from scrap yarn for one sleeve, cast on 0 (0, 3, 4, 4, 4) sts—50 (58, 66, 70, 76, 80) sts. Join for working in the rnd, pm.

SHAPE SLEEVES

SIZES 35 (39, 43½)

Work 7 rnds even.

DEC RND 1: K23 (27, 31), SSK, pm, k2tog, knit to end—48 (56, 64) sts rem.

Work 1 rnd even.

DEC RND 2: Knit to 2 sts before marker, SSK, k2tog, knit to end—46 (54, 62) sts rem.

Rep last 2 rnds 3 times more—40 (48, 56) sts rem.

SIZE 47½

DEC RND 1: K2tog, knit to last 2 sts, SSK—68 sts rem.

Work 3 rnds even.

Rep Dec Rnd 1 once more—66 sts rem.

Work 2 rnds even.

DEC RND 2: K31, SSK, pm, k2tog, knit to end—64 sts rem.

Work 1 rnd even.

Rep last 2 rnds 4 times more—56 sts rem.

SIZE 51

DEC RND 1: K2tog, knit to last 2 sts, SSK—74 sts rem.

Work 3 rnds even.

Rep Dec Rnd 1 once more—72 sts rem.

Work 2 rnds even.

DEC RND 2: K35 sts, SSK, pm, k2tog, knit to end—70 sts rem.

Rep Dec Rnd 1 once—68 sts rem.

Rep Dec Rnd 2 once—66 sts rem.

Work 1 rnd even.

Rep Dec Rnd 2 once—64 sts rem.

Rep Dec Rnd 1 once—62 sts rem.

Rep Dec Rnd 2 once—60 sts rem.

Work 1 rnd even.

Rep last 2 rnds once—58 sts rem.

SIZE 55

DEC RND 1: K2tog, knit to last 2 sts, SSK—78 sts rem.

Work 1 rnd even.

Rep last 2 rnds twice more—74 sts rem.

Work 1 rnd even.

DEC RND 2: K34 sts, SSK, pm, k2tog, knit to end—72 sts rem.

Rep Dec Rnd 1 once—70 sts rem.

Rep Dec Rnd 2 once—68 sts rem.

Work 1 rnd even.

Rep Dec Rnd 2 once—66 sts rem.

Rep Dec Rnd 1 once—64 sts rem.

Rep Dec Rnd 2 once—62 sts rem.

Work 1 rnd even.

Rep Dec Rnd 2 once—60 sts rem.

Rep Dec Rnd 1 once—58 sts rem.

ALL SIZES

NEXT RND: Change to size US 10½ (6.5mm) circular needle.

Work 1 rnd even.

INC RND: *K2 (2, 3, 3, 4, 4), M1; rep from * to last 0 (0, 2, 2, 2, 2) sts, k0 (0, 2, 2, 2, 2)—60 (72, 74, 74, 72, 72) sts.

Work 1 rnd even.

NEXT RND: Work 25 rnds in trim patt. Bind off purlwise.

FINISHING

Seam underarms.

NECK TRIM

With RS facing, using size US 7 needle, beg at right back shoulder, pick up and knit 1 st for each st cast on for back, sleeve and front, 4 sts for every inch (or 3cm) along left front neck edge, 1 st for each st cast on for front neck, 4 sts for every inch (or 3cm) along right front neck edge, and 1 st for each st cast on for front and sleeve, ending with an even number. Join for working in the rnd, pm.

Work 8 rnds in neck trim patt. Bind off purlwise.

Weave in ends.

LACE PANEL
TUNIC

The lace panels at the front and sleeves unite the long, lean line of this sweater with its blouson sleeves. The mohair and silk in this hand-dyed yarn add up to a lofty and soft garment that will hold its shape through several wears. This garment is knit from the top down, and set-in sleeves add structure to the delicate airiness of the lace.

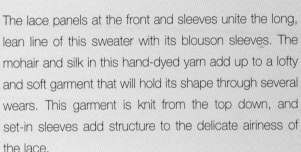

FINISHED MEASUREMENTS

BUST: 36¾ (41, 44¾, 49, 52¾)" (93 [104, 114, 124, 134]cm)

YARN

1 (1, 1, 2, 2) hanks (1100 yds [1005m] ea) Neighborhood Fiber Company Penthouse Silk Lace (100% silk)

  COLOR KALORAMA CIRCLE

6 (6, 7, 7, 8) hanks (170 yds [155m] ea) Neighborhood Fiber Company Loft (kid mohair/silk blend)

  COLOR KALORAMA CIRCLE

NEEDLES

size US 7 (4.5mm) 32" or 40" (81cm or 102cm) circular needle

size US 5 (3.75mm) 40" (102cm) circular needle

If necessary, change needle size to obtain correct gauge.

NOTIONS

stitch markers

scrap yarn

darning needle

GAUGE

22 sts and 28 rows = 4" (10cm) in St st, using larger needle

NOTES

PM (PLACE MARKER): Slip a premade marker or a loosely knotted piece of scrap yarn in a contrasting color onto the right-hand needle after the stitch just knit to mark a spot in the knitting to refer to on future rows. When you come to a marker, simply slip it from the right-hand needle to the left-hand needle.

[ ] (REPEAT OPERATION): Rep the bracketed operation the number of times indicated.

KFB (KNIT 1 FRONT AND BACK): Inc 1 st by knitting into the front and back of the next st.

SL MARKER OR SL ST(S) (SLIP MARKER OR SLIP STITCH[ES]): Slip a st or sts purlwise from the left needle to the right needle. When slipping a marker, knit the sts before and after it as usual.

M1 (MAKE 1): Inc 1 st by picking up the bar between the next st and the st just knit and knitting into it.

SSK (SLIP, SLIP, KNIT): Dec 1 st by slipping 2 sts knitwise one at a time, inserting the tip of the left needle into both sts and knitting the 2 sts tog.

K2TOG (KNIT 2 TOGETHER): Dec 1 st by knitting 2 sts tog.

RLI (RIGHT LIFTED INCREASE): Inc 1 st by inserting the tip of the right needle into the back of the st 1 row below on the left needle and knitting into it to create a right-leaning increase.

SEED STITCH

Work seed st over a multiple of 2 sts.

WORKED IN THE RND:

RND 1: *K1, p1; rep from * to last st, k1.

RND 2: *P1, k1; rep from * to last st, p1.

Rep Rnds 1–2.

WORKED FLAT:

ROW 1: *K1, p1; rep from * end.

ROW 2: *P1, k1; from * end.

Rep Rows 1–2.

YOKE

Using larger needle, cast on 70 (72, 72, 76, 76) sts. Do not join.

RAGLAN SET-UP ROW (WS): P1, pm, p14, pm, p40 (42, 42, 46, 46), pm, p14, pm, p1.

RAGLAN INC ROW 1 (RS): KFB, [KFB, knit to 1 st before marker, KFB] 3 times, KFB—78 (80, 80, 84, 84) sts.

Work 1 row even.

RAGLAN INC ROW 2 (RS): [Knit to 1 st before marker, KFB, sl marker, KFB] 4 times, knit to end—86 (88, 88, 92, 92) sts.

Work 1 row even.

Rep last 2 rows 6 times more—134 (136, 136, 140, 140) sts.

RAGLAN AND NECK INC ROW (RS): K2, M1, [knit to 1 st before marker, KFB, sl marker, KFB] 4 times, knit to last 2 sts, M1, k2—144 (146, 146, 150, 150) sts.

Work 1 row even.

Rep Raglan Inc Row 2 times—152 (154, 154, 158, 158) sts.

Work 1 row even.

Rep last 2 rows 3 (3, 2, 2, 2) times more—176 (178, 170, 174, 174) sts.

Rep last 10 (10, 8, 8, 8) rows 3 (3, 4, 4, 4) times more—302 (304, 306, 310, 310) sts.

Rep Raglan and Neck Inc Row—312 (314, 316, 320, 320) sts.

Work 1 row even.

Rep Raglan Inc Row 2 0 (1, 1, 2, 2) times more—312 (322, 324, 336, 336) sts.

Work 1 row even. Small sizes go on to body section.

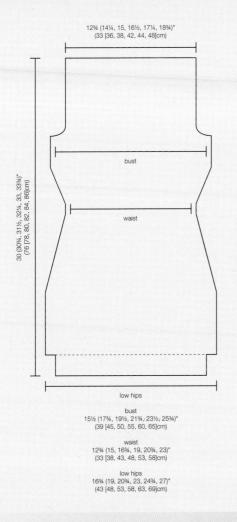

12¾ (14¼, 15, 16½, 17¼, 18¾)"
(33 [36, 38, 42, 44, 48]cm)

bust

waist

30 (30¾, 31½, 32¼, 33, 33¾)"
(76 [78, 80, 82, 84, 86]cm)

low hips

bust
15½ (17¾, 19½, 21¾, 23½, 25¾)"
(39 [45, 50, 55, 60, 65]cm)

waist
12¾ (15, 16¾, 19, 20¾, 23)"
(33 [38, 43, 48, 53, 58]cm)

low hips
16¾ (19, 20¾, 23, 24¾, 27)"
(43 [48, 53, 58, 63, 69]cm)

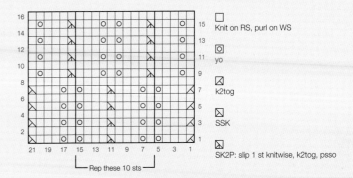

□ Knit on RS, purl on WS

⊡ yo

⊠ k2tog

⊠ SSK

⊠ SK2P: slip 1 st knitwise, k2tog, psso

└ Rep these 10 sts ┘

SIZES 41 (44¾, 49, 52¾)

Rep Raglan Inc Row—322 (324, 328, 328) sts.

Work 1 row even.

Rep last 2 rows 0 (0, 1, 1) time—322 (324, 336, 336) sts.

BODY

ALL SIZES

SEPARATE SLEEVES FROM BODY

NEXT ROW (RS): Work 35 (36, 37, 38, 38) sts, place next 72 (74, 74, 76, 76) sts for first sleeve on scrap yarn to be worked later, cast on 0 (4, 9, 12, 17) sts for underarm, pm, cast on 0 (4, 9, 12, 17) sts, work to next marker, place next 72 (74, 74, 76, 76) sts for second sleeve on scrap yarn to be worked later, cast on 0 (4, 9, 12, 17) sts, pm, cast on 0 (4, 9, 12, 17) sts, work 35 (36, 37, 38, 38) sts—168 (190, 212, 232, 252) sts. Do not join.

Work 5 (3, 3, 1, 1) rows even.

NECK INC ROW (RS): K2, M1, knit to last, 2 sts, M1, k2—170 (192, 214, 234, 254) sts.

Work 3 rows even.

Rep last 4 rows twice more—174 (196, 218, 238, 158) sts.

Rep Neck Inc Row—176 (198, 220, 240, 260) sts.

Work 1 row even.

Rep last 2 rows 7 (8, 7, 9, 9) times more—190 (214, 234, 258, 278) sts.

SHAPE WAIST

WAIST DEC AND NECK INC ROW (RS): Cast on 3 sts, [knit to 4 sts before marker, SSK, k4, k2tog] 2 times, knit to end, cast on 3 sts—192 (216, 236, 260, 280) sts.

Join for working in the rnd. Work 3 rnds even.

WAIST DEC RND: [Knit to 4 sts before marker, SSK, k4, k2tog] 2 times, knit to end—188 (212, 232, 256, 276) sts rem.

Work 3 rnds even.

Rep last 4 rnds 3 (3, 4, 4, 4) times more—176 (200, 216, 240, 260) sts rem.

WAIST INC RND: [Knit to 2 sts before marker, RLI, k4, RLI] 2 times—180 (204, 220, 244, 264) sts.

Work 3 rnds even.

Rep last 4 rnds 4 (4, 5, 5, 5) times more—196 (220, 240, 264, 284) sts.

Work 2 rnds even.

Rep Waist Inc Rnd—200 (224, 244, 268, 288) sts.

Work 5 rnds even.

Rep last 6 rnds 3 times more—212 (236, 256, 280, 300) sts.

Work even until piece measures 17 (17¼ 17½, 17¾, 18)" (43 [44, 44, 45, 46]cm) from underarm, inc 1 st on last rnd—213 (237, 257, 281, 301) sts.

NEXT RND: Work in seed st for 14 rnds. Bind off in patt.

SLEEVES

NEXT ROW: Cast on 0 (4, 9, 12, 17) sts, k72 (74, 74, 76, 76) sts from scrap yarn for 1 sleeve, cast on 0 (4, 9, 12, 17) sts—72 (82, 92, 100, 110) sts.

Purl 1 row.

NEXT ROW: Work in seed st for 10 rows. Bind off in patt.

FINISHING

Seam sleeves. Seam underarms.

NECK TRIM

With RS facing, using smaller needle and beg at back left raglan line, pick up and k10 sts along top of left sleeve, 50 (52, 50, 53, 58) sts along left side of front neck, pm, 50 (52, 50, 53, 58) sts along right side of front neck, 10 sts along top of right sleeve, and 29 (31, 31, 33, 35) sts along back neck—161 (167, 163, 171, 183) sts.

Join for working in the rnd, pm for beg of rnd.

RND 1 (DEC RND): Work in seed st to 2 sts before marker, SSK, k2tog, work in seed st to end—159, (165, 161, 169, 181) sts rem.

RND 2: Work in seed st to 2 sts before marker, k4, work in seed st to end.

Rep last 2 rnds 2 times more—155 (161, 157, 165, 179) sts rem.

Bind off in patt, working Rnd 1 on bind-off rnd.

Weave in ends.

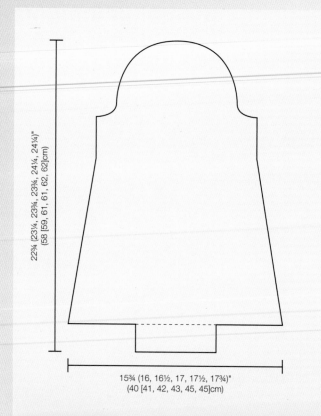

22¾ (23¼, 23¾, 24¼, 24¼)" (58 [59, 61, 61, 62]cm)

15¾ (16, 16½, 17, 17½, 17¾)" (40 [41, 42, 43, 45, 45]cm)

FITTED
DEEP-RIBBED CARDIGAN

This cardigan is completely structured, from the binary knit-and-purl stitch pattern to the set-in sleeves and side shaping. Knit in a cashmere blend, it has the softness of cashmere, the durability of wool and the loft of microfiber. For a daytime look, wear it with a pencil skirt and a white blouse. For evening, pair it with a silky cami.

FINISHED MEASUREMENTS

BUST: 34 (38, 42, 46, 50, 54)" (86 [97, 107, 117, 127, 137]cm), including front bands

YARN

10 (11, 13, 14, 15, 17) balls (88 yds [89m] ea) Cascade Yarns Cash Vero (extrafine merino wool/microfiber/cashmere blend)
COLOR MINT GREEN 16

NEEDLES

size US 8 (5mm) straight needles

size US 6 (4mm) straight needles

If necessary, change needle size to obtain correct gauge.

NOTIONS

7 ⅛" (3mm) buttons

darning needle

GAUGE

20 sts and 30 rows = 4" (10cm) in broken rib, using larger needles

NOTES

WORK 2 TOG (KNIT OR PURL 2 TOGETHER): Dec 1 st by knitting or purling 2 sts tog as one, in keeping with the est patt.

PM (PLACE MARKER): Slip a premade marker or a loosely knotted piece of scrap yarn in a contrasting color onto the right-hand needle after the stitch just knit to mark a spot in the knitting to refer to on future rows. When you come to a marker, simply slip it from the right-hand needle to the left-hand needle.

KFB (KNIT 1 FRONT AND BACK): Inc 1 st by knitting into the front and back of the next st.

P2TOG TBL (PURL 2 TOGETHER THROUGH BACK LOOP): Dec 1 st by inserting the needle into the backs of the next 2 sts and purling them tog.

P2TOG (PURL 2 TOGETHER): Dec 1 st by purling 2 sts tog.

K2TOG (KNIT 2 TOGETHER): Dec 1 st by knitting 2 sts tog.

SSK (SLIP, SLIP, KNIT): Dec 1 st by slipping 2 sts knitwise one at a time, inserting the tip of the left needle into both sts and knitting the 2 sts tog.

YO (YARN OVER): Wrap the working yarn around the needle clockwise and knit the next st as usual. This operation creates an eyelet hole in the knitting and inc 1 st.

BROKEN RIB

Work broken rib over a multiple of 2 sts.

ROW 1 (WS): *p1, k1; rep from * to end, end p1 if working odd number sts.

ROW 2: Knit.

Rep Rows 1–2.

BACK

With larger needles, cast on 91 (101, 111, 121, 131, 141) sts. Work in broken rib for 2" (5cm), ending with a WS row.

SHAPE WAIST

WAIST DEC ROW (RS): K1, work 2 tog, work to last 3 sts, work 2 tog, k1—89 (99, 109, 119, 129, 139) sts rem.

Work 3 rows even.

Rep last 4 rows 9 times more—71 (81, 91, 101, 111, 121) sts rem.

Work 3 rows even.

WAIST INC ROW (RS): K1, KFB, work to last 2 sts, KFB, k1—73 (83, 93, 103, 113, 123) sts.

Work 5 rows even.

Rep last 6 rows 6 times more—85 (95, 105, 115, 125, 135) sts.

Work even until piece measures 18 (18½, 19, 19½, 20, 20½)" [46 (47, 48, 50, 51, 52)cm] from beg, ending with a WS row.

SHAPE ARMHOLES

NEXT ROW (RS): Bind off 4 (5, 6, 7, 9, 11) sts at beg of next 2 rows—77 (85, 93, 101, 107, 113) sts rem.

NEXT ROW: K1, work 2 tog, work to last 3 sts, work 2 tog, k1—75 (83, 91, 99, 105, 111) sts rem.

Work 1 row even.

Rep last 2 rows 5 (6, 7, 8, 9, 10) times more—65 (71, 77, 83, 87, 91) sts rem.

Work even until armholes measure 5 (5½, 5¾, 6, 6, 6¼)" [13, (14, 15, 15, 15, 16)cm] from beg of shaping, ending with a WS row.

SHAPE NECK AND SHOULDERS

NEXT ROW (RS): Work 20 (23, 26, 29, 31, 33) sts, join a second ball of yarn, bind off center 25 sts, work to end.

NEXT ROW (WS): Working both sides at once with separate balls of yarn, on left neck edge, work to last 2 sts, p2tog tbl; on right neck edge, p2tog, work to end—19 (22, 25, 28, 30, 32) sts rem each side.

NEXT ROW: On right neck edge, work to last 2 sts, k2tog; on left neck edge, SSK, work to end—18 (21, 24, 27, 29, 31) sts rem each side.

Rep last 2 rows 3 times more—12 (15, 18, 21, 23, 25) sts rem each side.

Work even until piece measures 7½ (8, 8¼, 8½, 8½, 8¾)" [19 (20, 21, 22, 22, 22)cm] from beg of armhole shaping, ending with a WS row. Bind off in patt.

LEFT FRONT

With larger needles, cast on 44 (48, 54, 58, 64, 68) sts. Work in broken rib for 2" (5cm), ending with a WS row.

SHAPE WAIST

WAIST DEC ROW (RS): K1, work 2 tog, work to end—43 (47, 53, 57, 63, 67) sts rem.

Work 3 rows even.

Rep last 4 rows 9 times more—34 (38, 44, 48, 54, 58) sts rem.

Work 3 rows even.

WAIST INC ROW (RS): K1, KFB, work to end—35 (39, 45, 49, 55, 59) sts rem.

Work 5 rows even.

Rep last 6 rows 6 times more—41 (45, 51, 55, 61, 65) sts.

Work even until piece measures 18 (18½, 19, 19½, 20, 20½)" [46 (47, 48, 50, 51, 52)cm] from beg, ending with a WS row.

SHAPE ARMHOLE

NEXT ROW (RS): Bind off 4 (5, 6, 7, 9, 11) sts, work to end—37 (40, 45, 48, 52, 54) sts rem.

Work 1 row even.

DEC ROW (RS): K1, work 2 tog, work to end—36 (39, 44, 47, 51, 53) sts rem.

Work 1 row even.

Rep last 2 rows 5 (6, 7, 8, 9, 10) times more—31 (33, 37, 39, 42, 43) sts rem.

Work even until armhole measures 1½ (2, 1¾, 2, 1½, 1¾)" [4 (5, 5, 5, 4, 5)cm] from beg of shaping, ending with a RS row.

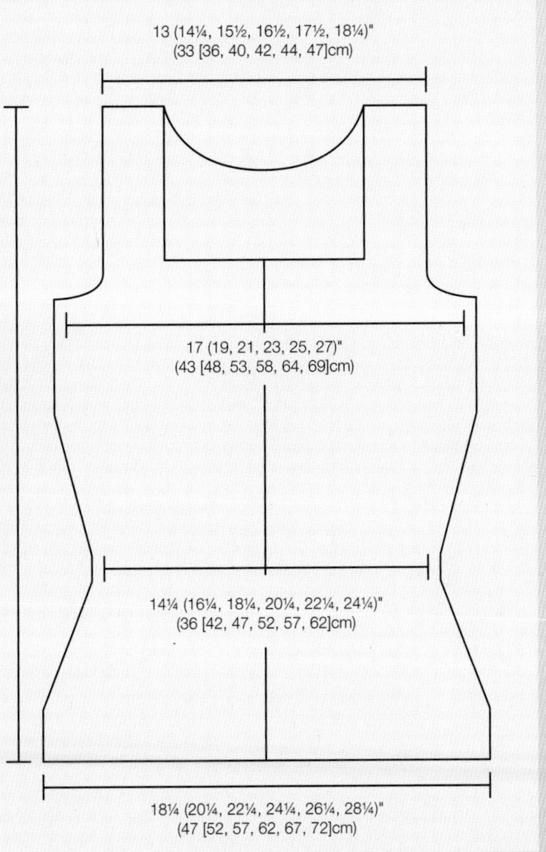

Schematic measurements:

13 (14¼, 15½, 16½, 17½, 18¼)" (33 [36, 40, 42, 44, 47]cm)

17 (19, 21, 23, 25, 27)" (43 [48, 53, 58, 64, 69]cm)

25½ (26½, 27¼, 28, 28½, 29¼)" (65 [67, 69, 71, 72, 74]cm)

14¼ (16¼, 18¼, 20¼, 22¼, 24¼)" (36 [42, 47, 52, 57, 62]cm)

18¼ (20¼, 22¼, 24¼, 26¼, 28¼)" (47 [52, 57, 62, 67, 72]cm)

SHAPE NECK

NEXT ROW (WS): Bind off 19 (18, 19, 18, 19, 18) sts, work to end—12 (15, 18, 21, 23, 25) sts rem.

Work even until piece measures 7½ (8, 8¼, 8½, 8½, 8¾)" [19 (20, 21, 22, 22, 22)cm] from beg of armhole shaping, ending with a WS row. Bind off in patt.

RIGHT FRONT

Work as for left front, reversing all shaping.

SLEEVES

With larger needles, cast on 42 (42, 42, 48, 48, 50) sts. Work in broken rib for 1" (3cm).

SHAPE SLEEVE

INC ROW (RS): K1, KFB, work to last 2 sts, KFB, k1—44 (44, 44, 50, 50, 52) sts.

Rep Inc Row every 12 (6, 6, 6, 6, 4) rows 2 (3, 12, 12, 14, 19) times more, then every 14 (8, 0, 0, 6, 0) rows 3 (6, 0, 0, 3, 0) times more—54 (62, 68, 74, 84, 90) sts.

Work even until piece measures 12½ (12½, 13, 13, 13½, 13½)" (32 [32, 33, 33, 34, 34]cm) from beg, ending with a WS row.

SHAPE CAP

NEXT ROW (RS): Bind off 4 (5, 6, 7, 9, 11) sts at beg of next 2 rows—46 (52, 56, 60, 66, 68) sts rem.

Work 20 (20, 22, 22, 24, 24) rows even.

DEC ROW (RS): K1, work 2 tog, work to last 3 sts, work 2 tog, k1—44 (50, 54, 58, 64, 66) sts rem.

Work 19 (21, 21, 23, 23, 23) rows even.

NEXT ROW (RS): Rep Dec Row once more—42 (48, 52, 56, 62, 64) sts rem.

Work 1 row even.

Rep last 2 rows 3 times more—36 (40, 44, 48, 56, 56) sts rem.

NEXT ROW (RS): *K2tog; rep from * to end—18 (20, 22, 24, 28, 28) sts rem.

NEXT ROW: *P2tog; rep from * to end—9 (10, 11, 12, 14, 14) sts rem.

Bind off loosely.

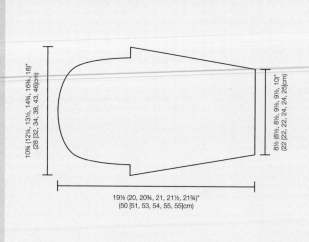

10¾ (12¼, 13½, 14¾, 16¾, 18)"
(28 [32, 34, 38, 43, 46]cm)

8½ (8½, 8½, 9½, 9½, 10)"
(22 [22, 22, 24, 24, 25]cm)

19½ (20, 20¾, 21, 21½, 21¾)"
(50 [51, 53, 54, 55, 55]cm)

FINISHING

Seam shoulders. Set in sleeves. Seam sides and sleeves.

BUTTON BAND

With RS facing, using smaller needles, pick up and knit 103 (107, 109, 113, 113, 117) sts along left front edge.

ROW 1 (WS): Purl.

ROWS 2–5: Work in St st.

ROW 6 (TURNING ROW) (RS): K1, *yo, k2tog; rep from * to end.

ROWS 7–12: Work in St st. Bind off loosely.

Fold the band at the turning row. Seam the bound-off edge to the pick-up row on the WS. Mark positions for 7 buttons, the first ½" (1cm) from the bottom edge, the last ½" (1cm) below the neck edge, with the rest evenly spaced between.

BUTTONHOLE BAND

Work as for button band, working buttonholes on Rows 3 and 9 as foll: *Work to buttonhole, yo, p2tog; rep from * to last buttonhole, work to end.

Attach buttons. Weave in ends.

ROMANTIC
BELL-SLEEVED CARDI

Knit from a beautiful double-stranded cashmere, this blouse is so soft and airy it actually feels a bit sinful. The garment is knit in one piece from the neckline to the hemline. The piping is a picot trim detail knit into the garment as you go, and the ruffle is created by changing to a larger needle and increasing a few stitches over one row.

FINISHED MEASUREMENTS

BUST: 32½ (36½, 40½, 44½, 48½, 52½)" (83 [93, 103, 113, 123, 133]cm)

YARN

4 (4, 5, 5, 5, 6) hanks (255 yds [230m] ea) Art Yarns Cashmere 2 (100% cashmere)
COLOR GRAY CS124

NEEDLES

size US 2 (2.75mm) straight needles

size US 5 (3.75mm) 32" or 40" (81cm or 102cm) circular needle

size US 8 (5mm) 32" or 40" (81cm or 102cm) circular needle

If necessary, change needle size to obtain correct gauge.

NOTIONS

stitch markers

scrap yarn

darning needle

sewing needle and thread

9 ¼" (6mm) shank buttons

GAUGE

24 sts and 32 rows = 4" (10cm) in St st, using size US 5 (3.75mm) needle

NOTES

PM (PLACE MARKER): Slip a premade marker or a loosely knotted piece of scrap yarn in a contrasting color onto the right-hand needle after the stitch just knit to mark a spot in the knitting to refer to on future rows. When you come to a marker, simply slip it from the right-hand needle to the left-hand needle.

[ ] (REPEAT OPERATION): Rep the bracketed operation the number of times indicated.

KFB (KNIT 1 FRONT AND BACK): Inc 1 st by knitting into the front and back of the next st.

SL MARKER OR SL ST(S) (SLIP MARKER OR SLIP STITCH[ES]): Slip a st or sts purlwise from the left needle to the right needle. When slipping a marker, knit the sts before and after it as usual.

P2TOG (PURL 2 TOGETHER): Dec 1 st by purling 2 sts tog.

YO (YARN OVER): Wrap the working yarn around the needle clockwise and knit the next st as usual.

K2TOG (KNIT 2 TOGETHER): Dec 1 st by knitting 2 sts tog.

M1 (MAKE 1): Inc 1 st by picking up the bar between the next st and the st just knit and knitting into it.

SSK (SLIP, SLIP, KNIT): Dec 1 st by slipping 2 sts knitwise one at a time, inserting the tip of the left needle into both sts and knitting the 2 sts tog.

WORK 2 TOG (KNIT OR PURL 2 TOGETHER): Dec 1 st by knitting or purling 2 sts tog as one, in keeping with the est patt.

SEED STITCH

Work seed st over a multiple of 2 sts + 1.

ALL ROWS: K1, *p1, k1; rep from * to end.

YOKE

With size US 5 (3.75mm) needle, cast on 124 (128, 128, 132, 136, 140) sts. Do not join.

RAGLAN SET-UP ROW (WS): P25 (26, 26, 27, 28, 30), pm, p12 (12, 12, 12, 10, 10), pm, p50 (52, 52, 54, 60, 60), pm, p12 (12, 12, 12, 10, 10), pm, p25 (26, 26, 27, 28, 30). Do not join.

RAGLAN INC ROW (RS): [Knit to 1 st before marker, KFB, sl marker, KFB] 4 times, knit to end—132 (136, 136, 140, 144, 148) sts.

NEXT ROW: Purl.

Rep last 2 rows 23 (26, 29, 32, 35, 38) times more—316 (344, 368, 396, 424, 452) sts.

BODY

SEPARATE SLEEVES FROM BODY

NEXT ROW (RS): K49 (53, 56, 60, 64, 69), place next 60 (66, 72, 78, 82, 88) sts for first sleeve on scrap yarn to be worked later, cast on 0 (4, 10, 14, 14, 20) sts for underam, knit to next marker, place next 60 (66, 72, 78, 82, 88) sts for second sleeve on scrap yarn to be worked later, cast on 0 (4, 10, 14, 14, 20) sts, k49 (53, 56, 60, 64, 69) sts—196 (220, 244, 268, 288, 316) sts. Do not join.

Work even until piece measures 5 (5¼, 5, 4¾, 4½, 4¼)" (13 [13, 13, 12, 11, 11]cm) from underarm, ending with a RS row.

Knit 2 rows, purl 1 row, knit 1 row.

PICOT ROW (WS): *P2tog, yo; rep from * to last 2 sts, p2tog—195 (219, 243, 267, 287, 315) sts rem.

Knit 1 row, purl 1 row.

NEXT ROW (RS): *K2tog (1 st from needle together with 1 st from back of sixth row below needle); rep from * to end.

Knit 1 row.

INC ROW (RS): Change to size US 8 (5mm) needle. *K4 (5, 6, 7, 8, 9), M1; rep from * to last 3 (4, 3, 8, 7, 9) sts, k3 (4, 3, 8, 7, 9)—243 (262, 283, 304, 322, 349) sts.

Purl 1 row.

NEXT ROW (RS): Work in dot st from chart on page 55 for 18 rows, beg first row with st# 6 (5, 1, 5, 5, 1).

NEXT ROW (RS): Work in seed st for 20 rows. Bind off in patt.

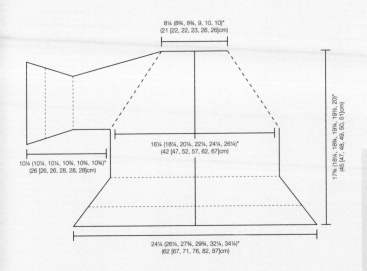

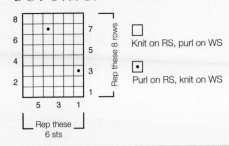

DOT STITCH

Knit on RS, purl on WS

• Purl on RS, knit on WS

Rep these 8 rows

Rep these 6 sts

Knit 1 row.

INC ROW (RS): Change to size US 8 (5mm) needle. *K4, M1; rep from * to last 3 (5, 3, 5, 3, 5) sts, k3 (5, 3, 5, 3, 5)—73 (80, 88, 95, 103, 110) sts.

Purl 1 row.

NEXT ROW (RS): Work in dot st from chart on this page for 18 rows, beg first row with st# 1 (1, 5, 5, 1, 1).

Beg with the next RS row, work in seed st for 20 rows. Bind off in patt.

FINISHING

Seam sleeves and underarms.

NECK TRIM

With RS facing, using US 5 (3.75mm) needle, beg at right front edge, pick up and knit 1 st for every cast-on st.

Purl 1 row, knit 1 row, purl 1 row.

PICOT ROW (RS): *K2tog, yo; rep from * to last 2 sts, k2tog.

Purl 1 row, knit 1 row.

NEXT ROW (WS): *P2tog (1 st from pick-up row together with 1 st from needle); rep from * to end. Bind off.

BUTTON BAND

With RS facing, using US 2 (2.75mm) needle, pick up and knit 109 (111, 115, 119, 121, 125) sts along left front edge. Work 2 rows in seed st. Bind off in patt.

BUTTONHOLE BAND

With RS facing, using US 2 (2.75mm) needle, pick up and knit 109 (111, 115, 119, 121, 125) sts along left front edge. Place 9 markers for buttonholes, evenly spaced.

NEXT ROW (WS): Work in seed st to marker, [yo, work 2 tog, work to next marker] 8 times, yo, work 2 tog, work to end.

Work 1 row in seed st. Bind off in patt.

Weave in ends.

Attach buttons with sewing needle and thread.

SLEEVES

NEXT ROW (RS): Cast on 0 (2, 5, 7, 7, 10) sts, k60 (66, 72, 78, 82, 88) from scrap yarn for 1 sleeve, cast on 0 (2, 5, 7, 7, 10) sts—60 (70, 82, 92, 96, 108) sts.

Purl 1 row.

SHAPE SLEEVE

SIZES 36½ (40½, 44½, 48½, 52½)

DEC ROW (RS): K1, SSK, knit to last 3 sts, k2tog, k1—68 (80, 90, 94, 106) sts rem.

Work 7 (7, 3, 5, 3) rows even.

Rep last 8 (8, 4, 6, 4) rows 1 (4, 1, 4, 7) time(s) more—66 (72, 88, 86, 92) sts rem.

Rep Dec Row 0 (0, 1, 1, 1) time more—66 (72, 86, 84, 90) sts rem. Work 1 (1, 5, 1, 1) rows even.

SIZE 44½

Rep Dec Row once more—84 sts rem.

Work 5 rows even.

Rep last 6 rows 3 times more—78 sts rem.

ALL SIZES

Work even until piece measures 5 (5, 5, 5½, 5½, 5½)" (13 [13, 13, 14, 14, 14]cm) from underarm, ending with a RS row.

Knit 2 rows, purl 1 row, knit 1 row.

PICOT ROW (WS): *P2tog, yo; rep from * to last 2 sts, p2tog—59 (65, 71, 77, 83, 89) sts rem.

Knit 1 row, purl 1 row.

NEXT ROW (RS): *K2tog (1 st from needle tog with 1 st from back of sixth row below needle); rep from * to end.

DRESSED TO KILL
SKIRTS AND DRESSES

Another trend I love is layering dresses with pants, over a knit tank dress or over a contrasting slip. Most of the dresses in this chapter incorporate a lace pattern so any layers underneath are visible. Textures really vary among these garments—from the decadent white eyelet lace dress (see page 62) to the straightforward mohair-and-silk tunic dress (see page 66).

SILK SKIRT

This skirt is made to coordinate with the *Silk Cami* on page 18. Like the camisole, the skirt is worked in two silk yarns, Pure and Simple and Disco Lights. The skirt is worked from the hemline up to the waist. The waistband is folded and conceals a length of elastic to ensure a proper fit. Granted, a silk skirt isn't something you'll wear every day, though you'll probably want to! This is a quick knit, so why not try one in hemp, tweed or a cotton blend?

FINISHED MEASUREMENTS

WAIST: 24 (28, 32, 36, 40, 44)" (61 [71, 81, 91, 102, 112]cm)

HIPS: 40 (44, 48, 52, 56, 60)" (102 [112, 122, 132, 142, 152]cm

YARN

2 (3, 3, 3, 3, 4) hanks (260 yds [234m] ea) Tilli Tomas Pure and Simple (100% spun silk)
COLOR GLAMPYRE (MC)

2 (2, 2, 2, 2, 3) hanks (225 yds [203m] ea) Tilli Tomas Disco Lights (spun silk/petite sequins blend)
COLOR SAPPHIRE (CC)

NEEDLES

2 size US 6 (4mm) 24", 29", 32" or 40" (61cm, 74cm, 81cm or 102cm) circular needles

If necessary, change needle size to obtain correct gauge.

NOTIONS

¾ (1, 1, 1, 1¼, 1¼) yd(s) (.75 [.75, 1, 1, 1.25, 1.25]m) ½" (2cm) wide elastic

size US G-6 (4mm) crochet hook

1 ¾" (2cm) button

GAUGE

24 sts and 30 rows = 4" (10cm) in St st

NOTES

YO (YARN OVER): Wrap the working yarn around the needle clockwise and knit the next st as usual. This operation creates an eyelet hole in the knitting and inc 1 st.

SK2P (SLIP 1, KNIT 2 TOGETHER, PASS SLIPPED STITCH OVER): Dec 2 sts by knitting 2 sts tog and passing the slipped st over the st rem after the 2 sts were knit tog.

[ ] (REPEAT OPERATION): Rep the bracketed operation the number of times indicated.

PM (PLACE MARKER): Slip a premade marker or a loosely knotted piece of scrap yarn in a contrasting color onto the right-hand needle after the stitch just knit to mark a spot in the knitting to refer to on future rows. When you come to a marker, simply slip it from the right-hand needle to the left-hand needle.

M1 (MAKE 1): Inc 1 st by picking up the bar between the next st and the st just knit and knitting into it.

SL MARKER OR SL ST(S) (SLIP MARKER OR SLIP STITCH[ES]): Slip a st or sts purlwise from the left needle to the right needle. When slipping a marker, knit the sts before and after it as usual.

FISHTAIL LACE

Work fishtail lace over a multiple of 8 sts.

RND 1 (RS): *K1, yo, k2, SK2P, k2; rep from * around.

RNDS 2 AND 4: Knit.

RND 3: *K2, yo, k1, SK2P, k1, yo, k1; rep from * around.

RND 5: *K3, yo, SK2P, yo, k2; rep from * around.

RND 6: Knit.

Rep Rnds 1–6.

BODY

WAIST CASING

Cast on 144 (168, 192, 216, 240, 264) sts. Work in St st for 7 rows, beg with a purl row.

NEXT ROW (TURNING ROW) (RS): Purl.

Work in St st for 8 rows.

NEXT ROW (WS): [P36 (42, 48, 54, 60, 66) sts, pm] 4 times.

JOIN FOR BODY

INC RND: With RS facing, join for working in the rnd, pm. [K1, M1, knit to 1 st before marker, M1, k1, sl marker] 4 times—152 (176, 200, 224, 248, 272) sts.

Work 3 rnds even.

Rep last 4 rnds 11 times more—240 (264, 288, 312, 336, 360) sts.

Work even until piece measures 13 (13¼, 13½, 13¾, 14¼, 14¾)" (33 [34, 34, 35, 36, 38]cm) from turning row. Set aside.

LACE TRIM

With spare circular needle, cast on 240 (264, 288, 312, 336, 360) sts. Join for working in the rnd, pm. Work in fishtail lace for 36 rnds (6 vertical patt rep). Using Kitchener st (see page 140 in the Special Techniques Glossary), graft sts to body sts.

FINISHING

Fold the casing at the turning row and seam it to the WS, leaving 1" (3cm) unsewn at 1 end. Measure your waist; cut the elastic to 1" (3cm) shorter than your waist measurement. Insert the elastic into the casing and seam the rem edges of the casing, making sure to catch the ends of the elastic when seaming the side edges. With RS facing and using a crochet hook, work a crochet chain button loop at the left edge of the casing. Sew a button opposite the button loop.

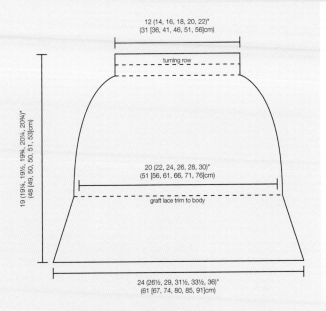

12 (14, 16, 18, 20, 22)"
(31 [36, 41, 46, 51, 56]cm)

turning row

19 (19¼, 19½, 19¾, 20¼, 20¾)"
(48 [49, 50, 50, 51, 53]cm)

20 (22, 24, 26, 28, 30)"
(51 [56, 61, 66, 71, 76]cm)

graft lace trim to body

24 (26½, 29, 31½, 33½, 36)"
(61 [67, 74, 80, 85, 91]cm)

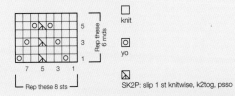

Rep these
6 rnds

5

1

7 5 3 1

Rep these 8 sts

☐ knit

☐ yo

⊠ SK2P: slip 1 st knitwise, k2tog, psso

LACE
MINI-DRESS

Knit from a yarn that is an incredible combination of two luxe fibers (angora and alpaca), this lace dress is a showstopper. The lace is floaty and airy, but the set-in sleeves and side seams provide structure to the garment. I chose to knit mine in a demure white, but it would look great in black or even red as well. This is a layering piece, and I love to wear mine over a dark tank dress or a slip with tights and Mary Jane heels.

FINISHED MEASUREMENTS
BUST: 34½ (37½, 40½, 43½, 47, 50, 53)"
(88 [95, 103, 110, 119, 127, 135]cm)

YARN
4 (4, 5, 5, 6, 6, 7) balls (98 yds [88m] ea)
Cascade Yarns Cash Vero (extrafine merino wool/microfiber/cashmere blend)
COLOR WHITE 003

NEEDLES
size US 6 (4mm) straight needles

size US 8 (5mm) straight needles

size US 6 (4mm) 29" (74cm) circular needle

size US 8 (5mm) 29" (74cm) circular needle

If necessary, change needle size to obtain correct gauge.

NOTIONS
stitch holders

15 ½" (1cm) shank buttons

GAUGE
20½ sts and 24 rows = 4" (10cm) in grand eyelets patt, using larger needles

NOTES

YO (YARN OVER): Wrap the working yarn around the needle clockwise and knit the next st as usual. This operation creates an eyelet hole in the knitting and inc 1 st.

P4TOG (PURL 4 TOGETHER): Dec 3 sts by purling 4 sts tog.

SSK (SLIP, SLIP, KNIT): Dec 1 st by slipping 2 sts knitwise one at a time, inserting the tip of the left needle into both sts and knitting the 2 sts tog.

K2TOG (KNIT 2 TOGETHER): Dec 1 st by knitting 2 sts tog.

SEED STITCH

Work seed st over a multiple of 2 sts.

ROW 1: *K1, p1; rep from * end.

ROW 2: *P1, k1; from * end.

Rep Rows 1–2.

GRAND EYELETS PATTERN

Work grand eyelets patt over a multiple of 4 sts.

NOTE: *When working shaping, do not work a dec within grand eyelets patt without a corresponding inc and vice versa.*

ROW 1: P2, *yo, p4tog; rep from * to last 2 sts, p2.

ROW 2: K3, [k1, p1, k1] into next st, *k1, [k1, p1, k1] into next st; rep from * to last 2 sts, k2.

ROW 3: Knit.

Rep Rows 1–3.

NOTE: *Because this is a 3-row rep, Row 1 will be alternately a RS and then a WS row.*

BACK AND FRONT

With smaller needles, cast on 96 (104, 112, 120, 128, 136, 144) sts. Work in seed st for 2½" (6cm).

Change to larger needles. Work in grand eyelets patt until piece measures 3¼" (8cm) from beg, ending with a WS row.

SHAPE WAIST

NEXT ROW (RS): K1, SSK, work to last 3 sts, k2tog, k1—94 (102, 110, 118, 126, 134, 142) sts rem.

Work 25 (25, 27, 27, 29, 29, 31) rows even.

Rep last 26 (26, 28, 28, 30, 30, 32) rows 3 times more—88 (96, 104, 112, 120, 128, 136) sts rem.

Work even until piece measures 20 (20½, 21, 21½, 22, 22½, 23)" (51 [52, 53, 55, 56, 57, 58]cm) from beg, ending with a WS row.

SHAPE ARMHOLES

NEXT ROW (RS): Bind off 4 (5, 6, 7, 8, 9, 10) sts at beg of next 2 rows—80 (86, 92, 98, 104, 110, 116) sts rem.

DEC ROW (RS): K1, SSK, work to last 3 sts, k2tog, k1—78 (84, 90, 96, 102, 108, 114) sts rem.

Work 1 row even.

Rep last 2 rows 5 (6, 7, 8, 9, 10, 11) times more—68 (72, 76, 80, 84, 88, 92) sts rem.

Work even until armholes measure 5¾ (5¾, 6¼, 6¼, 6½, 6½, 6¾)" (15 [15, 16, 16, 17, 17, 17]cm) from beg of shaping, ending with a WS row.

SHAPE NECK

Beg on a RS row, work 21 (23, 24, 26, 27, 29, 30) sts, place center 26 (26, 28, 28, 30, 30, 32) sts on holder, join a second ball of yarn, work to end. Working both sides at once with separate balls of yarn, work 1 row even.

DEC ROW (RS): On first side of neck, work to last 2 sts, k2tog; on second side of neck, SSK, work to end—20 (22, 23, 25, 26, 28, 29) sts rem each side.

Work 1 row even.

Rep last 2 rows 7 times more—13 (15, 16, 18, 19, 21, 22) sts rem each side.

Work even until armholes measure 8 (8, 8½, 8½, 8¾, 8¾, 9)" (20 [20, 22, 22, 22, 22, 23]cm) from beg of shaping, ending with a WS row.

SHAPE SHOULDERS

NEXT ROW (RS): Bind off 6 (7, 8, 9, 9, 10, 11) sts at beg of next 2 rows, then 7 (8, 8, 9, 10, 11, 11) sts at beg of next 2 rows.

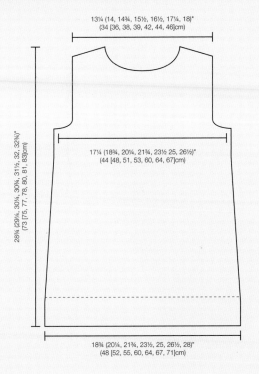

13¼ (14, 14¾, 15½, 16½, 17¼, 18)"
(34 [36, 38, 39, 42, 44, 46]cm)

28¾ (29¼, 30¼, 30¾, 31½, 32, 32¾)"
(73 [75, 77, 78, 80, 81, 83]cm)

17¼ (18¾, 20¼, 21¾, 23½ 25, 26½)"
(44 [48, 51, 53, 60, 64, 67]cm)

18¾ (20¼, 21¾, 23½, 25, 26½, 28)"
(48 [52, 55, 60, 64, 67, 71]cm)

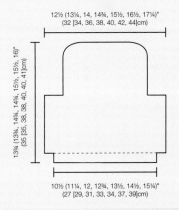

12½ (13¼, 14, 14¾, 15½, 16½, 17¼)"
(32 [34, 36, 38, 40, 42, 44]cm)

13¾ (13¾, 14¾, 14¾, 15½, 15½, 16)"
(35 [35, 38, 38, 40, 40, 41]cm)

10½ (11¼, 12, 12¾, 13½, 14½, 15¼)"
(27 [29, 31, 33, 34, 37, 39]cm)

SLEEVES

With smaller needles, cast on 52 (56, 60, 64, 68, 72, 76) sts. Work even in seed st for 1" (3cm), inc 12 sts evenly across last WS row—64 (68, 72, 76, 80, 84, 88) sts.

NEXT ROW (RS): Change to larger needles. Work in grand eyelets patt until piece measures 7 (7, 7½, 7½, 8, 8, 8½)" (18 [18, 19, 19, 20, 20, 22]cm) from the beg, ending with a WS row.

SHAPE CAP

NEXT ROW (RS): Bind off 4 (5, 6, 7, 8, 9, 10) sts at beg of next 2 rows—56 (58, 60, 62, 64, 66, 68) sts rem.

Work even until cap measures 5½ (5½, 6, 6, 6¼, 6¼, 6¼)" (14 [14, 15, 15, 16, 16, 16]cm) from beg of shaping, ending with a WS row.

DEC ROW (RS): K1, k2tog, work to last 3 sts, SSK, k1—54 (56, 58, 60, 62, 64, 66) sts rem.

Work 1 row even.

Rep last 2 rows 3 times more—48 (50, 52, 54, 56, 58, 60) sts rem. Bind off loosely.

FINISHING

Seam shoulders. Set in sleeves, gathering bound-off sts at top of sleeve so that top is only 3" (8cm) wide. Seam sides and sleeves.

COLLAR

With RS facing, using smaller circular needle, beg at center of front neck, knit across 13 (13, 14, 14, 15, 15, 16) sts from holder for front neck, pick up and knit 18 sts along right front neck edge, 18 sts along right back neck edge, knit across 26 (26, 28, 28, 30, 30, 32) sts from holder for back neck, pick up and knit 18 sts along left back neck edge, 18 sts along left front neck edge and knit across 13 (13, 14, 14, 15, 15, 16) sts from holder for front neck—124 (124, 128, 128, 132, 132, 136) sts.

Work in seed st for ½" (1cm). Change to larger circular needle. Work in seed st until piece measures 3" (8cm). Bind off loosely in patt.

Attach 4 buttons to the center of each sleeve. Attach 7 buttons to the center front.

Weave in ends.

DEEP U-NECK
TUNIC DRESS

This dress is knit from a yarn containing two strands: One strand is a deliciously soft mohair, and the other is a rich silk. Both strands are individually dyed, making the color variation striking but not overpowering. The dress is simply knit from the neckline down to the hem, with only the neckline trim being picked up and knit on later. The dress incorporates bust and side shaping for a perfect fit.

FINISHED MEASUREMENTS

BUST: 36¾ (41, 44¾, 49, 52¾)" (93 [104, 114, 124, 134]cm)

YARN

4 (4, 5, 5, 5) hanks (260 yds [234m] ea) Art Yarns Silk Rhapsody (100% silk stranded with mohair/silk blend)
COLOR TURQUOISE 107

NEEDLES

size US 7 (4.5mm) 32" or 40" (81cm or 102cm) circular needle

size US 5 (3.75mm) 40" (102cm) circular needle

If necessary, change needle size to obtain correct gauge.

NOTIONS

stitch markers

scrap yarn

darning needle

GAUGE

22 sts and 28 rows = 4" (10cm) in St st, using larger needle

NOTES

PM (PLACE MARKER): Slip a premade marker or a loosely knotted piece of scrap yarn in a contrasting color onto the right-hand needle after the stitch just knit to mark a spot in the knitting to refer to on future rows. When you come to a marker, simply slip it from the right-hand needle to the left-hand needle.

KFB (KNIT 1 FRONT AND BACK): Inc 1 st by knitting into the front and back of the next st.

[ ] (REPEAT OPERATION): Rep the bracketed operation the number of times indicated.

SL MARKER OR SL ST(S) (SLIP MARKER OR SLIP STITCH[ES]): Slip a st or sts purlwise from the left needle to the right needle. When slipping a marker, knit the sts before and after it as usual.

M1 (MAKE 1): Inc 1 st by picking up the bar between the next st and the st just knit and knitting into it.

SSK (SLIP, SLIP, KNIT): Dec 1 st by slipping 2 sts knitwise one at a time, inserting the tip of the left needle into both sts and knitting the 2 sts tog.

K2TOG (KNIT 2 TOGETHER): Dec 1 st by knitting 2 sts tog.

RLI (RIGHT LIFTED INCREASE): Inc 1 st by inserting the tip of the right needle into the back of the st 1 row below on the left needle and knitting into it to create a right-leaning increase.

SEED STITCH

Work seed st over a multiple of 2 sts.

WORKED IN THE RND:

RND 1: *K1, p1; rep from * to last st, k1.

RND 2: *P1, k1; rep from * to last st, p1.

Rep Rnds 1–2.

WORKED FLAT:

ROW 1: *K1, p1; rep from * end.

ROW 2: *P1, k1; rep from * end.

Rep Rows 1–2.

YOKE

Using larger needle, cast on 70 (72, 72, 76, 76) sts. Do not join.

RAGLAN SET-UP ROW (WS): P1, pm, p14, pm, p40 (42, 42, 46, 46), pm, p14, pm, p1.

RAGLAN INC ROW 1 (RS): KFB, [KFB, knit to 1 st before marker, KFB] 3 times, KFB—78 (80, 80, 84, 84) sts.

Work 1 row even.

RAGLAN INC ROW 2 (RS): [Knit to 1 st before marker, KFB, sl marker, KFB] 4 times, knit to end—86 (88, 88, 92, 92) sts.

Work 1 row even.

Rep last 2 rows 6 times more—134 (136, 136, 140, 140) sts.

RAGLAN AND NECK INC ROW (RS): K2, M1, [knit to 1 st before marker, KFB, sl marker, KFB] 4 times, knit to last 2 sts, M1, k2—144 (146, 146, 150, 150) sts.

Work 1 row even.

Rep Raglan Inc Row 2—152 (154, 154, 158, 158) sts.

Work 1 row even.

Rep last 2 rows 3 (3, 2, 2, 2) times more—176 (178, 170, 174, 174) sts.

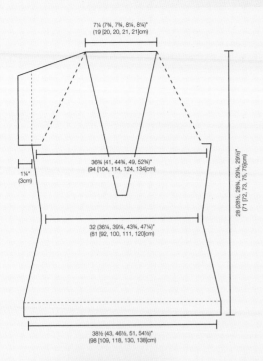

Figure measurements:
- 7¼ (7¾, 7¾, 8¼, 8¼)" (19 [20, 20, 21, 21]cm)
- 36¾ (41, 44¾, 49, 52¾)" (94 [104, 114, 124, 134]cm)
- 1¼" (3cm)
- 32 (36¼, 39¼, 43¾, 47¼)" (81 [92, 100, 111, 120]cm)
- 28 (28½, 28¾, 29¼, 29½)" (71 [72, 73, 75, 75]cm)
- 38½ (43, 46½, 51, 54½)" (98 [109, 118, 130, 138]cm)

Rep last 10 (10, 8, 8, 8) rows 3 (3, 4, 4, 4) times more—302 (304, 306, 310, 310) sts.

Rep Raglan and Neck Inc Row—312 (314, 316, 320, 320) sts. Work 1 row even.

Rep Raglan Inc Row 2 0 (1, 1, 2, 2) times more—312 (322, 324, 336, 336) sts.

Work 1 row even. Smallest size go on to body section.

SIZES 41 (44¾, 49, 52¾)

Rep Raglan Inc Row—322 (324, 328, 328) sts.

Work 1 row even.

Rep last 2 rows 0 (0, 1, 1) time—322 (324, 336, 336) sts.

BODY

ALL SIZES

SEPARATE SLEEVES FROM BODY

NEXT ROW (RS): Work 35 (36, 37, 38, 38) sts, place next 72 (74, 74, 76, 76) sts for first sleeve on scrap yarn to be worked later, cast on 0 (4, 9, 12, 17) sts for underarm, pm, cast on 0 (4, 9, 12, 17) sts, work to next marker, place next 72 (74, 74, 76, 76) sts for second sleeve on scrap yarn to be worked later, cast on 0 (4, 9, 12, 17) sts, pm, cast on 0 (4, 9, 12, 17) sts, work 35 (36, 37, 38, 38) sts—168 (190, 212, 232, 252) sts. Do not join.

Work 5 (3, 3, 1, 1) rows even.

NECK INC ROW (RS): K2, M1, knit to last, 2 sts, M1, k2—170 (192, 214, 234, 254) sts.

Work 3 rows even.

Rep last 4 rows twice more—174 (196, 218, 238, 158) sts.

Rep Neck Inc Row—176 (198, 220, 240, 260) sts.

Work 1 row even.

Rep last 2 rows 7 (8, 7, 9, 9) times more—190 (214, 234, 258, 278) sts.

SHAPE WAIST

WAIST DEC AND NECK INC ROW (RS): Cast on 3 sts, [knit to 4 sts before marker, SSK, k4, k2tog] 2 times, knit to end, cast on 3 sts—192 (216, 236, 260, 280) sts. Join for working in the rnd, pm.

Work 3 rnds even.

WAIST DEC RND: [Knit to 4 sts before marker, SSK, k4, k2tog] 2 times, knit to end—188 (212, 232, 256, 276) sts rem.

Work 3 rnds even.

Rep last 4 rnds 3 (3, 4, 4, 4) times more—176 (200, 216, 240, 260) sts rem.

WAIST INC RND: [Knit to 2 sts before marker, RLI, k4, RLI] 2 times—180 (204, 220, 244, 264) sts.

Work 3 rnds even.

Rep last 4 rnds 4 (4, 5, 5, 5) times more—196 (220, 240, 264, 284) sts.

Work 2 rnds even.

Rep Waist Inc Rnd—200 (224, 244, 268, 288) sts.

Work 5 rnds even.

Rep last 6 rnds 3 times more—212 (236, 256, 280, 300) sts.

Work even until piece measures 17 (17¼, 17½, 17¾, 18)" (43 [44, 44, 45, 46]cm) from underarm, inc 1 st on last rnd—213 (237, 257, 281, 301) sts.

NEXT RND: Work in seed st for 14 rnds. Bind off in patt.

SLEEVES

NEXT ROW: Cast on 0 (4, 9, 12, 17) sts, k72 (74, 74, 76, 76) sts from scrap yarn for 1 sleeve, cast on 0 (4, 9, 12, 17) sts—72 (82, 92, 100, 110) sts.

Purl 1 row. Work in seed st for 10 rows. Bind off in patt.

FINISHING

Seam sleeves. Seam underarms.

NECK TRIM

With RS facing, using smaller needle and beg at back left raglan line, pick up and k10 sts along top of left sleeve, 50 (52, 50, 53, 58) sts along left side of front neck, pm, 50 (52, 50, 53, 58) sts along right side of front neck, 10 sts along top of right sleeve, and 29 (31, 31, 33, 35) sts along back neck—161 (167, 163, 171, 183) sts. Join for working in the rnd, pm for beg of rnd.

RND 1 (DEC RND): Work in seed st to 2 sts before marker, SSK, k2tog, work in seed st to end—159, (165, 161, 169, 181) sts rem.

RND 2: Work in seed st to 2 sts before marker, k4, work in seed st to end.

Rep last 2 rnds 2 times more—155 (161, 157, 165, 179) sts rem.

Bind off in patt, working Rnd 1 on bind-off rnd.

Weave in ends.

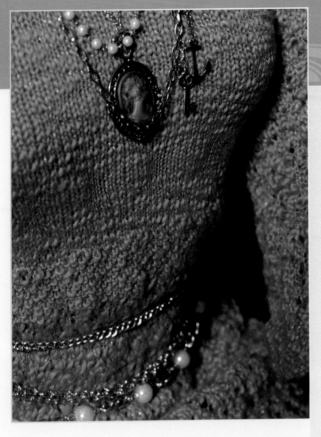

GOLD METALLIC
DRESS

Vegas, the yarn used in this dress, combines three of my favorite things: soy, wool and sparkle! How can you possibly go wrong? This dress is knit in the round from the neckline to the hemline, incorporating a simple, three-stitch lace pattern in the sleeves and skirt. This dress is perfect for layering and would look great over a thin cotton dress, contrast-colored slip or even jeans!

FINISHED MEASUREMENTS

BUST: 33 (37, 41, 45, 49, 52½)" (84 [94, 104, 114, 124, 133]cm)

YARN

6 (7, 8, 8, 9, 10) balls (109 yds [98m] ea) South West Trading Company Vegas (wool/Soysilk®/metallic thread blend)
COLOR 424 FLYING ELVIS

NEEDLES

size US 6 (4mm) 32" or 40" (81cm or 102cm) circular needle

size US 8 (5mm) 32" or 40" (81cm or 102cm) circular needle

If necessary, change needle size to obtain correct gauge.

NOTIONS

stitch markers

scrap yarn

darning needle

GAUGE

21 sts and 28 rows = 4" (10cm) in St st, using smaller needle

NOTES

YO (YARN OVER): Wrap the working yarn around the needle clockwise and knit the next st as usual. This operation creates an eyelet hole in the knitting and inc 1 st.

SK2P (SLIP 1, KNIT 2 TOGETHER, PASS SLIPPED STITCH OVER): Dec 2 sts by knitting 2 sts tog and passing the slipped st over the st rem after the 2 sts were knit tog.

PM (PLACE MARKER): Slip a premade marker or a loosely knotted piece of scrap yarn in a contrasting color onto the right-hand needle after the stitch just knit to mark a spot in the knitting to refer to on future rows. When you come to a marker, simply slip it from the right-hand needle to the left-hand needle.

[ ] (REPEAT OPERATION): Rep the bracketed operation the number of times indicated.

KFB (KNIT 1 FRONT AND BACK): Inc 1 st by knitting into the front and back of the next st.

SL MARKER OR SL ST(S) (SLIP MARKER OR SLIP STITCH[ES]): Slip a st or sts purlwise from the left needle to the right needle. When slipping a marker, knit the sts before and after it as usual.

SEED STITCH

Work seed st over a multiple of 2 sts + 1.

RND 1: *K1, p1; rep from * to last st, k1.

RND 2: *P1, k1; rep from * to last st, p1.

Rep Rnds 1–2.

TRELLIS LACE

Work trellis lace over a multiple of 6 sts.

RND 1 (RS): *K3, yo, SK2P, yo; rep from * to end.

RND 2: Knit.

RND 3: *Yo, SK2P, yo, k3; rep from * to end.

RND 4: Knit.

Rep Rows 1–4.

YOKE

With smaller needle, cast on 77 (79, 81, 83, 85, 87) sts. Do not join.

RAGLAN SET-UP ROW (WS): P7 (7, 8, 8, 9, 10), pm, p14, pm, p35 (37, 37, 39, 39, 39), pm, p14, pm, p7 (7, 8, 8, 9, 10).

RAGLAN INC ROW (RS): [Knit to 1 st before marker, KFB, sl marker, KFB] 4 times, knit to end—85 (87, 89, 91, 93, 95) sts.

Work 1 row even.

Rep last 2 rows 24 (26, 28, 29, 30, 31) times more—277 (295, 313, 323, 333, 343) sts.

SHAPE FRONT NECK

NEXT ROW (RS): Rep Raglan Inc Row, cast on 21 (23, 23, 25, 25, 25) sts at end of row. Join for working in the rnd—306 (326, 344, 356, 366, 376) sts.

NOTE: *Consider first sleeve marker the beg of the rnd marker from now on.*

Work 1 rnd even.

SEPARATE SLEEVES FROM BODY

NEXT RND (RS): Place next 66 (70, 74, 76, 78, 80) sts for first sleeve on scrap yarn to be worked later (do not remove first sleeve marker), cast on 0 (4, 10, 16, 24, 30) sts for underarm, knit to marker, place next 66 (70, 74, 76, 78, 80) sts for second sleeve on scrap yarn to be worked later, cast on 0 (4, 10, 16, 24, 30) sts, knit to end—174 (194, 216, 236, 258, 276) sts.

BODY

Work 6" (15cm) even in St st. Work 2" (5cm) even in seed st, dec 0 (2, 0, 2, 0, 0) sts on last rnd—174 (192, 216, 234, 258, 276) sts rem.

NEXT RND: Change to larger needle. Work in trellis lace (see written pattern, this page, or charted pattern, page 75, for reference) until piece measures 24½ (25, 25½, 26, 26½, 27)" (62 [64, 65, 66, 67, 69]cm) from underarm, dec 1 st on last rnd—173 (191, 215, 233, 257, 275) sts rem.

NEXT RND: Work 1" (3cm) in seed st. Bind off in patt.

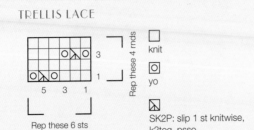

TRELLIS LACE

☐ knit

☐ yo

◪ SK2P: slip 1 st knitwise, k2tog, psso

Rep these 4 rnds

Rep these 6 sts

5 3 1

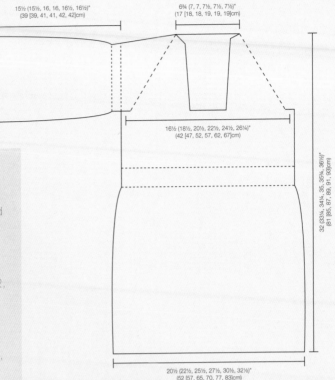

15½ (15½, 16, 16, 16½, 16½)"
(39 [39, 41, 41, 42, 42]cm)

6¾ (7, 7, 7½, 7½, 7½)"
(17 [18, 18, 19, 19, 19]cm)

16½ (18½, 20½, 22½, 24½, 26¼)"
(42 [47, 52, 57, 62, 67]cm)

32 (33¼, 34¼, 35, 35¾, 36½)"
(81 [85, 87, 89, 91, 93]cm)

20½ (22½, 25½, 27½, 30½, 32½)"
(52 [57, 65, 70, 77, 83]cm)

SLEEVES

NEXT RND: Transfer 66 (70, 74, 76, 78, 80) held sts of 1 sleeve to needle, cast on 0 (4, 10, 16, 24, 30) sts at end of needle for underarm—66 (74, 84, 92, 102, 110) sts. Join for working in the rnd, pm for beg of rnd.

Work 1" (3cm) even in seed st, inc 1 st on first rnd and dec 1 (3, 0, 3, 0, 3) sts on last rnd—66 (72, 84, 90, 102, 108) sts rem.

Change to larger needle. Work in trellis lace (see written pattern, page 74, or charted pattern, this page, for reference) until piece measures 14½ (14½, 15, 15, 15½, 15½)" (37 [37, 38, 38, 39, 39]cm) from underarm.

NEXT RND: Work 1" (3cm) in seed st. Bind off in patt.

FINISHING

Seam underarms.

NECK TRIM

With RS facing and beg at back right raglan line, pick up and knit 24 (25, 25, 27, 27, 27) sts along back neck, 10 sts along top of left sleeve, 5 (5, 6, 6, 7, 9) sts along top left of front neck, pm 27 (29, 31, 32, 33, 34) sts along left side of front neck, pm, 15 (16, 16, 18, 18, 18) sts along bottom center of front neck, pm, 27 (29, 31, 32, 33, 34) sts along right side of front neck, pm, 5 (5, 6, 6, 7, 9) sts along top right of front neck, and 10 sts along top of right sleeve. Join for working in the rnd, pm for beg of rnd.

Work 1" (3cm) in seed st, inc 1 st on either side of markers at top of front neck, and dec 1 st on either side of markers at bottom center of front neck on every rnd.

Bind off in patt. Weave in ends.

OVER THE TOP
SHRUGS, WRAPS AND JACKETS

The toppers in this chapter run the gamut from long and bold to short and sweet. There's everything from a knee-length coat (see page 110) that will really turn heads to a subtly rich *Textured Circle Shrug* (see page 82) knit from luscious hand-dyed merino that's the perfect accent to a summer dress. Whatever the weather, and whatever your mood, you'll find an outer garment here for every occasion.

LACY DOLMAN

When you think of angora sweaters, images of 1940s and 1950s pinup girls may come to mind. But an angora sweater doesn't have to be ultra-tight and super-fluffy. This updated version is more free-flowing, but still delicate thanks to the lacework on the top and sleeves. This cardigan is so lightweight you'll feel like you're wearing cotton candy…and draw attention like flies to honey. While this cardigan may look difficult, it's actually formed from two rectangles bordered with simple ribbing.

FINISHED MEASUREMENTS

TO FIT WAIST: 24–26 (28–30, 32–34, 36–38, 40–42, 44–46)" (61–66 [71–76, 81–86, 91–97, 102–107, 112–117]cm)

WAIST: 21 (25, 29, 32, 35, 38)" (53 [64, 74, 81, 89, 97]cm)

NOTE: *Ribbing will stretch to fit waist measurements.*

YARN

9 (10, 11, 13, 14, 15) hanks (50 yds [45m] ea) Lorna's Laces Angel (angora/lambswool blend)
COLOR BLACKBERRY

NEEDLES

size US 10½ (6.5mm) straight needles

size US 6 (4mm) 29 (74cm) circular needle

If necessary, change needle size to obtain correct gauge.

NOTIONS

stitch markers

darning needle

4 ⅝" (2cm) buttons

GAUGE

11 sts and 14 rows = 4" (10cm) in lace ladder, using larger needle

NOTES

K2TOG (KNIT 2 TOGETHER): Dec 1 st by knitting 2 sts tog.

YO (YARN OVER): Wrap the working yarn around the needle clockwise and knit the next st as usual. This operation creates an eyelet hole in the knitting and inc 1 st.

[ ] (REPEAT OPERATION): Rep the bracketed operation the number of times indicated.

SSK (SLIP, SLIP, KNIT): Dec 1 st by slipping 2 sts knitwise one at a time, inserting the tip of the left needle into both sts and knitting the 2 sts tog.

PM (PLACE MARKER): Slip a premade marker or a loosely knotted piece of scrap yarn in a contrasting color onto the right-hand needle after the stitch just knit to mark a spot in the knitting to refer to on future rows. When you come to a marker, simply slip it from the right-hand needle to the left-hand needle.

LACE LADDER

Work lace ladder over a multiple of 4 sts.

ROW 1 (RS): *K2tog, [yo] twice, SSK; rep from * to end.

ROW 2: *K1, [k1, p1] into double yo, k1; rep from * to end.

Rep Rows 1 and 2.

BODY/SLEEVE (MAKE 2)

With larger needles, cast on 52 (56, 64, 68, 76, 80) sts. Knit 1 row.

NEXT ROW (RS): Work in lace ladder for 24 (24½, 25, 25½, 26½, 27)" (61 [62, 64, 65, 67, 69]cm), ending with a RS row.

Knit 1 row. BO loosely.

FINISHING

Fold body/sleeve pieces in half lengthwise, with WS tog. Seam the 2 pieces together along 1 side edge, beg at bound-off edge of each piece and ending at fold line. Pm 31 (31, 35, 35, 39, 39) sts in from each open side along cast-on and bound-off edge of pieces. Seam sleeves, from outside edge to marker, sewing cast-on to bound-off edge.

RIBBING

With smaller needle, beg at center front, pick up and knit 86 (102, 118, 130, 142, 154) sts along open bottom edge of right front, back, then left front. Work in p2, k2 rib for 5" (13cm).

BO all loosely in patt.

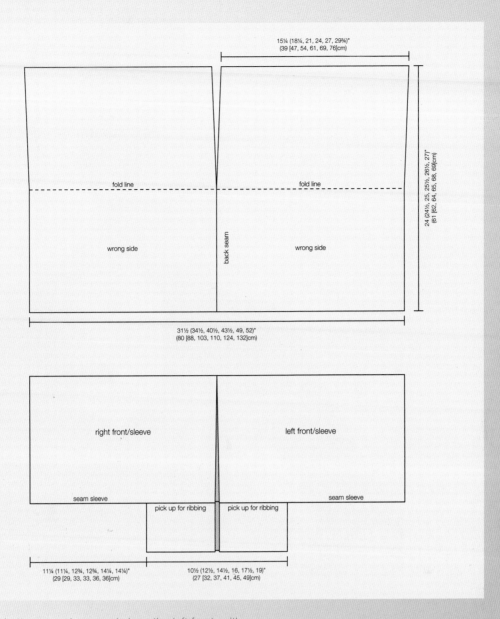

Attach 4 buttons evenly spaced along the left front, with the first button at the top edge of the ribbing, and the last button ½" (1cm) up from the bottom edge. The rem 2 buttons should be evenly spaced between the top and bottom buttons. Using a single strand of yarn and a darning needle, work 4 button loops along the right front, opposite the buttons. Work each loop by running a strand of yarn from the WS to the RS and then back to the WS a few rows below where the yarn came up, leaving just enough room to fit the button through the loop. Tie the ends of the loop, making sure the loop lies flat on the RS and does not bunch the fabric.

Weave in ends. Block if desired.

S

TEXTURED CIRCLE
SHRUG

Texture is the name of the game in this merino wool shrug. I combine several simple stitch patterns, such as garter ridges, ribbing on two different scales and seed stitch, to create a visual bang. This shrug follows the same basic construction as the traditional "raglan from the top down" sweater, without working any front panels. The ribbing is picked up all around the edges and worked in the round. The yarn is a gorgeous hand-dyed multistrand merino wool—the perfect choice for showing off the texture of the stitches.

FINISHED MEASUREMENTS

TO FIT BUST: 32–34 (36–38, 40–42, 44–46, 48–50, 52-54)" (81–86 [91–97, 102–107, 112–117, 122–127, 132–137]cm)

YARN

9 (11, 12, 15, 17, 19) hanks (98 yds [88m] ea) Neighborhood Fiber Co. Studio Worsted Semisolid Merino (100% superwash merino) **COLOR LOGAN CIRCLE**

NEEDLES

size US 8 (5mm) 29" (74cm) circular needle

size US 6 (4mm) 40" (102cm) circular needle

If necessary, change needle size to obtain correct gauge.

NOTIONS

stitch markers

scrap yarn

darning needle

GAUGE

18 sts and 26 rows = 4" (10cm) in textured stripe, using larger needle

NOTES

PM (PLACE MARKER): Slip a premade marker or a loosely knotted piece of scrap yarn in a contrasting color onto the right-hand needle after the stitch just knit to mark a spot in the knitting to refer to on future rows. When you come to a marker, simply slip it from the right-hand needle to the left-hand needle.

REV ST ST (REVERSE STOCKINETTE ST): Purl every row.

KFB (KNIT 1 FRONT AND BACK): Inc 1 st by knitting into the front and back of the next st.

[ ] (REPEAT OPERATION): Rep the bracketed operation the number of times indicated.

PFB (PURL 1 FRONT AND BACK): Inc 1 st by purling into the front and back of the next st.

K2TOG (KNIT 2 TOGETHER): Dec 1 st by knitting 2 sts tog.

P2TOG (PURL 2 TOGETHER): Dec 1 st by purling 2 sts tog.

SSK (SLIP, SLIP, KNIT): Dec 1 st by slipping 2 sts knitwise one at a time, inserting the tip of the left needle into both sts and knitting the 2 sts tog.

RLI (RIGHT LIFTED INCREASE): Inc 1 st by inserting the tip of the right needle into the back of the st 1 row below on the left needle and knitting into it to create a right-leaning increase.

SL MARKER OR SL ST(S) (SLIP MARKER OR SLIP STITCH[ES]): Slip a st or sts purlwise from the left needle to the right needle. When slipping a marker, knit the sts before and after it as usual.

M1P (MAKE 1 PURLWISE): Inc 1 st by picking up the bar between the next st and the st just knit and purling it.

TEXTURED STRIPE

Work textured stripe over any number of sts.

ROWS 1–5: Work in Rev St st.

ROWS 6–13: Work in St st.

Rep Rows 1–13.

NOTE: Because this is a 13-row rep, Row 1 will be alternately a RS and then a WS row.

SEED STITCH

Work seed st over a multiple of 2 sts + 1.

RND 1: *P1, k1; rep from * to last st, p1.

RND 2: *K1, p1; rep from * to last st, k1.

Rep Rnds 1–2.

YOKE

With larger needle, cast on 60 (60, 60, 68, 68, 68) sts. Do not join.

RAGLAN SET-UP ROW (WS): Beg St st, beg with a purl row. P10 (10, 10, 11, 11, 11), pm, p40 (40, 40, 46, 46, 46), pm p10 (10, 10, 11, 11, 11).

RAGLAN INC ROW (RS): [KFB, work to 1 st before marker, KFB] twice, KFB, work to last st, KFB—66 (66, 66, 74, 74, 74) sts.

Work 1 row even.

Rep last 2 rows 5 times more—96 (96, 96, 104, 104, 104) sts.

NEXT ROW (RS): Begin textured stripe and, at the same time, rep Raglan Inc Row every other row 14 (18, 22, 23, 27, 31) times more, working PFB instead of KFB when Raglan Inc Row is worked on a purl row—180 (204, 228, 242, 266, 290) sts.

Work 1 row even. Break yarn.

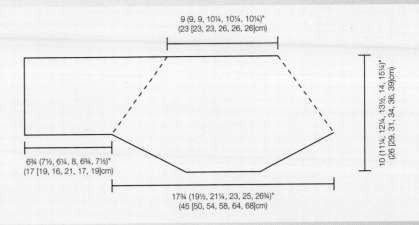

9 (9, 9, 10¼, 10¼, 10¼)"
(23 [23, 23, 26, 26, 26]cm)

10 (11¼, 12¼, 13½, 14, 15¼)"
(26 [29, 31, 34, 36, 39]cm)

6¾ (7½, 6¼, 8, 6¾, 7½)"
(17 [19, 16, 21, 17, 19]cm)

17¾ (19½, 21¼, 23, 25, 26¾)"
(45 [50, 54, 58, 64, 68]cm)

SEPARATE SLEEVES FROM BODY

NEXT ROW (RS): Place next 50 (58, 66, 69, 77, 85) sts for first sleeve on scrap yarn to be worked later, rejoin yarn and work to marker, place last 50 (58, 66, 69, 77, 85) sts for second sleeve on scrap yarn to be worked later—80 (88, 96, 104, 112, 120) sts rem.

Work 1 row even.

NEXT ROW (RS): Cont in textured stripe, bind off 3 sts at beg of next 10 (8, 0, 16, 0, 0) rows, then 4 sts at beg of next 6 (8, 14, 4, 16, 16) rows—26 (32, 40, 40, 48, 56) sts rem.

Place sts on scrap yarn to be worked later.

SLEEVES

NEXT ROW (RS): Transfer 50 (58, 66, 69, 77, 85) held sts of one sleeve to larger needle.

Cont in textured stripe, work even for 2 rows.

SIZES 40–42 (44–46, 48–50, 52–54)

DEC ROW (RS): Work 1, k2tog (p2tog if working a purl row), work to last 3 sts, SSK (p2tog if working a purl row), work 1—64 (67, 75, 83) sts rem.

Work 9 (21, 5, 3) rows even.

Rep last 10 (22, 6, 4) rows 2 (1, 5, 9) times more, then rep Dec Row 1 time more—58 (63, 63, 63) sts rem.

ALL SIZES

Work even until piece measures 6¾ (7½, 6¼, 8, 6¾, 7½)" (17 [19, 16, 20, 17, 19]cm) from beg, ending with first 5 rows of textured stripe. Bind off.

NECK TRIM

With RS facing, beg at right back bottom edge, using smaller needle, pick up and knit sts for ribbing around entire edge as foll:

Pick up and k34 (36, 34, 40, 40, 40) sts along right back edge, pm, 54 (62, 70, 74, 80, 90) sts along right sleeve, pm, 40 (40, 42, 46, 48, 46) sts along back neck, pm, 54 (62, 70, 74, 80, 90) sts along left sleeve, pm, 34 (36, 34, 40, 40, 40) sts along left back edge, k26 (32, 40, 40, 48, 56) sts from scrap yarn for lower back—242 (268, 290, 314, 336, 362) total sts.

Pm and join for working in the rnd. Work 33 (37, 41, 44, 48, 50) rnds in k1, p1 rib.

INC RND 1: Work to first marker, *[k1, p1, RLI, p1] 13 (15, 17, 18, 20, 22) times, [k1, p1] 1 (1, 1, 1, 0, 1) time, sl marker, work to next marker; rep from * once—268 (298, 324, 350, 376, 406) sts.

NEXT RND: Work to first marker, [k1, p1, k2, p1] 13 (15, 17, 18, 20, 22) times, [k1, p1] 1 (1, 1, 1, 0, 1) time, sl marker, work to next marker; rep from * once.

Work 12 (16, 20, 23, 27, 29) rnds even.

INC RND 2: Work to first marker, *[k1, p1, k1, M1P, k1] 13 (15, 17, 18, 20, 22) times, [k1, p1] 1 (1, 1, 1, 0, 1) time, sl marker, work to next marker; rep from * once—294 (328, 258, 286, 416, 450) sts.

NEXT RND: Work in seed st, inc 1 st at end of rnd—295 (329, 259, 287, 417, 451) sts.

Work 22 (22, 22, 26, 26, 26) rnds even. Bind off in patt.

FINISHING

Seam sleeves. Weave in ends.

KIMONO WRAP

There's something really satisfying about knitting lace with bulky yarn—lace knit at this gauge creates a truly striking visual impact, and it's quick, too. This piece is knit in one piece from the back hem over the shoulders to the fronts, with stitches for the borders and collars picked up at the end. The wide seed stitch borders at hem, neck and sleeve anchor the lace in a solid texture and provide structure that makes this garment very versatile and wearable. I love this kimono over a ribbed turtleneck dress with tall boots. It's also great over flowy cottons and, of course, with jeans and a simple tee.

FINISHED MEASUREMENTS

TO FIT BUST: 35½ (40, 44½, 48½, 53, 57½)" (90 [102, 113, 123, 135, 146]cm)

YARN

11 (12, 13, 14, 15, 16) hanks (65 yds [59m] ea) Malabrigo Yarn Gruesa (100% wool)

COLOR 143 TORERO

NEEDLES

size US 15 (10mm) 40" or 60" (102cm or 153cm) circular needle

size US 15 (10mm) straight needles

If necessary, change needle size to obtain correct gauge.

NOTIONS

stitch markers

darning needle

GAUGE

11 sts and 13 rows = 4" (10cm) in feather lace

NOTES

YO (YARN OVER): Wrap the working yarn around the needle clockwise and knit the next st as usual. This operation creates an eyelet hole in the knitting and inc 1 st.

K2TOG TBL (KNIT 2 TOGETHER THROUGH BACK LOOP): Dec 1 st by inserting the needle into the backs of the next 2 sts and knitting them tog.

K2TOG (KNIT 2 TOGETHER): Dec 1 st by knitting 2 sts tog.

SK2P (SLIP 1, KNIT 2 TOGETHER, PASS SLIPPED STITCH OVER): Dec 2 sts by slipping 1 st, knitting 2 sts tog and passing the slipped st over the st rem after the 2 sts were knit tog.

YF (WITH YARN IN FRONT): Move the working yarn to the front of the needle.

[ ] (REPEAT OPERATION): Rep the bracketed operation the number of times indicated.

PM (PLACE MARKER): Slip a premade marker or a loosely knotted piece of scrap yarn in a contrasting color onto the right-hand needle after the stitch just knit to mark a spot in the knitting to refer to on future rows. When you come to a marker, simply slip it from the right-hand needle to the left-hand needle.

RLI (RIGHT LIFTED INCREASE): Inc 1 st by inserting the tip of the right needle into the back of the st 1 row below on the left needle and knitting into it to create a right-leaning increase.

LLI-P (LEFT LIFTED INCREASE PURLWISE): Inc 1 st by inserting the tip of the right needle into the back of the st 1 row below on the left needle and purling.

RLI-P (RIGHT LIFTED INCREASE PURLWISE): Inc 1 st by inserting the tip of the right needle into the back of the st 1 row below on the left needle and purling.

FEATHER LACE

Work feather lace over a multiple of 6 sts + 1.

ROW 1 (RS): K1, *yo, k2tog tbl, k1, k2tog, yo, k1; rep from * to end.

ROW 2 AND ALL WS ROWS: Purl.

ROW 3: K1, *yo, k1, SK2P, k1, yf, k1; rep from * to end.

ROW 5: K1, *k2tog, yo, k1, yo, k2tog-tbl, k1; rep from * to end.

ROW 7: K2tog, *[k1, yo] twice, k1, SK2P; rep from * to last 5 sts, [k1, yo] twice, k1, k2tog-tbl.

ROW 8: Rep Row 2.

Rep Rows 1–8.

SEED STITCH

Work seed st over a multiple of 2 sts.

ROW 1 (WS): *K1, p1; rep from * to end.

ROW 2: *P1, k1; rep from * to end.

Rep Rows 1–2.

BODY

With circular needle, cast on 49 (55, 61, 67, 73, 79) sts. Work in feather lace until piece measures 25" (64cm) from beg, ending with Row 8 of patt. Pm at each edge for end of back.

SEPARATE FRONTS

NEXT ROW (RS): Cont in patt as est, work 22 (25, 28, 31, 34, 37) sts, join a second ball of yarn, bind off center 5 sts, work to end.

Working both sides at same time, work even until piece measures 25" (64cm) from markers, ending with Row 8 of patt. Bind off.

SLEEVES

With straight needles, cast on 10 sts. Work in seed st until piece measures 20" (51cm) from beg. Bind off in patt.

FINISHING

Seam sides, from bottom edge to 10" (25cm) below markers. Seam cast-on and bound-off edges of sleeves. Sew in sleeves, with sleeve seam at base of armhole.

BOTTOM BAND

With RS facing, using circular needle, beg at bottom left front, pick up and knit 88 (100, 112, 122, 132, 144) sts around entire bottom edge. Work in seed st for 6 (6, 6½, 6½, 7, 7)" (15 [15, 17, 17, 18, 18]cm). Bind off in patt.

FRONT AND NECK BANDS AND COLLAR

With RS facing, using circular needle, beg just above bottom band on right front, and end just above bottom band on left front, pick up and knit 118 sts along right front, back neck, and left front. Work in seed st for 2" (5cm), ending with a WS row.

NEXT ROW (RS): Bind off 26 sts in patt at beg of next 2 rows—66 sts rem.

NEXT ROW (RS): Work in p2, k2 rib for 1" (3cm), ending with a WS row.

INC ROW 1 (RS): Work 22 sts, [RLI] twice, work to last 24 sts, [RLI] twice, work to end—70 sts.

Work 1 row even, purling inc sts.

INC ROW 2 (RS): Work 23 sts, LLI-P, RLI-P, work to last 24 sts, LLI-P, RLI-P, work to end—74 sts.

Work 2 rows even, knitting inc sts on first row.

NEXT ROW (WS): Work in seed st for 2" (5cm). Bind off in patt.

Weave in ends.

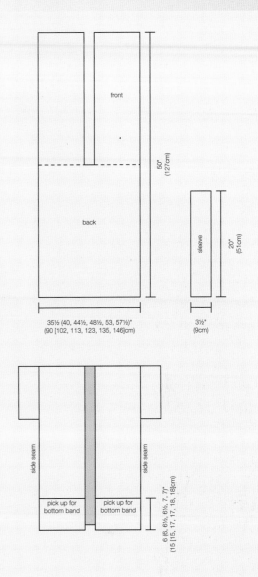

front

back

50" (127cm)

sleeve

20" (51cm)

35½ (40, 44½, 48½, 53, 57½)" (90 [102, 113, 123, 135, 146]cm)

3½" (9cm)

side seam

side seam

pick up for bottom band

pick up for bottom band

6 (6, 6½, 6½, 7, 7)" (15 [15, 17, 17, 18, 18]cm)

DOUBLE-BREASTED
CARDIGAN

This alpaca-and-wool half-and-half blend yarn gives you the softness and halo of alpaca combined with the resiliency of wool. Fitted at the high bust, this cardigan evolves into an easygoing shape at the body. Simple seed stitch contrasts with the firmer broken rib stitch of the upper part of the garment. The body and sleeves are knit from the top down in one piece. Ribbed lace panels are picked up from one front hemline, around the back of the neck, and down the other front. I love this cardigan over empire-waist dresses or long tunics.

FINISHED MEASUREMENTS

TO FIT BUST: 34–36 (38–40, 42–44, 46–48, 50–52)" (86–91 [97–102, 107–112, 117–122, 127–132]cm)

YARN

15 (17, 19, 21, 24) hanks (110 yds [99m] ea) Cascade Yarns Lana D'Oro (alpaca/wool blend)

COLOR GRAY 1050

NEEDLES

size US 5 (3.75mm) 40" or 60" (102cm or 152cm) circular needle

size US 7 (4.5mm) 40" (102cm) circular needle

If necessary, change needle size to obtain correct gauge.

NOTIONS

stitch markers

scrap yarn

6 ⅞" (2cm) buttons

GAUGE

18 sts and 31 rows = 4" (10cm) in broken rib, using larger needle

18 sts and 34 rows = 4" (10cm) in seed st, using larger needle

NOTES

K2TOG (KNIT 2 TOGETHER): Dec 1 st by knitting 2 sts tog.

[ ] (REPEAT OPERATION): Rep the bracketed operation the number of times indicated.

YO (YARN OVER): Wrap the working yarn around the needle clockwise and knit the next st as usual. This operation creates an eyelet hole in the knitting and inc 1 st.

SKP (SLIP 1, KNIT 1, PASS SLIPPED STITCH OVER): Dec 1 st by passing the first sl st over the knit st.

PM (PLACE MARKER): Slip a premade marker or a loosely knotted piece of scrap yarn in a contrasting color onto the right-hand needle after the stitch just knit to mark a spot in the knitting to refer to on future rows. When you come to a marker, simply slip it from the right-hand needle to the left-hand needle.

KFB (KNIT 1 FRONT AND BACK): Inc 1 st by knitting into the front and back of the next st.

SL MARKER OR SL ST(S) (SLIP MARKER OR SLIP STITCH[ES]): Slip a st or sts purlwise from the left needle to the right needle. When slipping a marker, knit the sts before and after it as usual.

BROKEN RIB

Work broken rib over a multiple of 2 sts.

ROW 1 (RS): Knit.

ROW 2: *P1, k1; rep from * to end.

Rep Rows 1–2.

SEED STITCH

Work seed st over a multiple of 2 sts.

ROW 1 (WS): *P1, k1; rep from * to end.

ROW 2: *K1, p1; rep from * to end.

Rep Rows 1–2.

LARGE EYELET RIB

Work large eyelet rib over a multiple of 6 sts +2.

ROW 1 (WS): K2, *p4, k2; rep from * to end.

ROW 2: P2, *k2tog, [yo] twice, SKP, p2; rep from * to end.

ROW 3: K2, *p1, k1, p2, k2; rep from * to end.

ROW 4: P2, *k4, p2; rep from * to end.

Rep Rows 1–4.

YOKE

With larger needle, cast on 60 (64, 66, 70, 74) sts. Do not join.

RAGLAN SET-UP ROW (WS): P2, pm, p10, pm, p36 (40, 42, 46, 50), pm p10, pm, p2.

Knit 1 row, purl 1 row.

RAGLAN INC ROW (RS): Working in broken rib, [work to 1 st before marker, KFB, sl marker, KFB] 4 times, work to end—68 (72, 74, 78, 82) sts.

Work 1 row even.

Rep last 2 rows 23 (13, 12, 7, 9) times—252 (176, 170, 134, 154) sts.

SIZES 34–36

Work 1 row even. Break yarn.

SIZES 38–40

RAGLAN AND NECK INC ROW (RS): KFB, [work to 1 st before marker, KFB, sl marker, KFB] 4 times, work to last st, KFB—186 sts.

Work 1 row even.

Rep Raglan Inc Row once more—194.

Work 1 row even.

Rep last 2 rows 10 times more—274 sts.

Rep Raglan and Neck Inc Row once more—284 sts.

Work 1 row even. Break yarn.

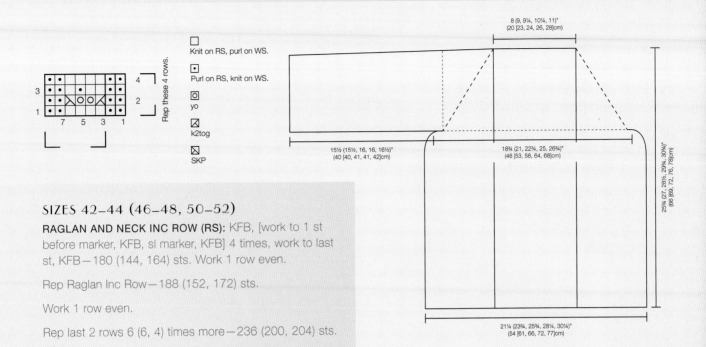

Chart Legend

☐ Knit on RS, purl on WS.

⊡ Purl on RS, knit on WS.

Ⓞ yo

⊠ k2tog

⊠ SKP

Rep these 4 rows.

SIZES 42–44 (46–48, 50–52)

RAGLAN AND NECK INC ROW (RS): KFB, [work to 1 st before marker, KFB, sl marker, KFB] 4 times, work to last st, KFB—180 (144, 164) sts. Work 1 row even.

Rep Raglan Inc Row—188 (152, 172) sts.

Work 1 row even.

Rep last 2 rows 6 (6, 4) times more—236 (200, 204) sts.

Rep Raglan and Neck Inc Row once more—246 (210, 214) sts.

Work 1 row even.

Rep last 16 (16, 12) rows 1 (2, 3) times more—312 (342, 364) sts.

Work 1 row even. Break yarn.

BACK

SEPARATE SLEEVES FROM BODY

ALL SIZES

NEXT ROW (WS): Place next 58 (64, 70, 76, 80) sts for first sleeve on scrap yarn to be worked later, join yarn, cast on 0 (2, 4, 6, 8) sts for underarm, work to marker, place next 58 (64, 70, 76, 80) sts for second sleeve on scrap yarn to be worked later, cast on 0 (2, 4, 6, 8) sts, work to end—136 (160, 180, 202, 220) sts.

NEXT ROW (RS): Knit 1 row, inc 5 sts evenly spaced to first marker, 12 sts evenly spaced to second marker, and 5 sts evenly spaced to end—158 (182, 202, 224, 242) sts.

NEXT ROW (WS): Work in seed st until piece measures 18 (18½, 19, 19½, 20)" (46 (47, 48, 50, 51]cm) from underarm, ending with a WS row.

Bind off in patt.

SLEEVES

NEXT ROW (WS): Cast on 0 (1, 2, 3, 4) sts, k58 (64, 70, 76, 80) sts from scrap yarn for one sleeve, cast on 0 (1, 2, 3, 4) sts—58 (66, 74, 82, 88) sts.

NEXT ROW (RS): Knit 1 row, inc 15 (11, 7, 3, 0) sts evenly spaced across row—73 (77, 81, 85, 88) sts.

NEXT ROW (WS): Work in seed st until piece measures 15½ (15½, 16, 16, 16½)" (39 [39, 41, 41, 42]cm) from underarm, ending with a WS row.

Bind off in patt.

FINISHING

Seam sleeves. Seam underarms.

NECK TRIM

With RS facing and using smaller needle, pick up and knit 6 sts per 1" (3cm) around entire neckline, beg at bottom right front and ending at bottom left front, ending with a multiple of 6 sts + 2.

NEXT ROW (WS): Work in large eyelet rib for 5 (5, 5½, 5½, 6)" (13 [13, 14, 14, 15]cm), ending with Row 4.

Bind off in patt.

Attach buttons to left front in pairs, 1" (3cm) in from either edge of trim, the first pair just above beg of seed st, and rem pairs spaced approximately 2¼" (6cm) apart. Push buttons through trim on right front.

TRAPEZE
JACKET

The foundation of this jacket is knit from the top down on one circular needle. The lacy trim is knit from the bottom up and attached later, allowing for the decorative cast-on edge of the lace to shape the hemlines of the body and the sleeves. The colors in this variegated yarn are rich, reminiscent of Monet's lily ponds. Wear this cozy jacket to complement those transitional outfits in the first days of fall and spring.

FINISHED MEASUREMENTS

BUST: 34 (39½, 44, 49, 55½)" (86 [100, 112, 124, 141]cm)

YARN

7 (8, 9, 10, 11) hanks (65 yds [59m] ea) Malabrigo Aquarella (100% wool)
COLOR 16 INDY

NEEDLES

size US 13 (9mm) 32" or 40" (81cm or 102cm) circular needle

If necessary, change needle size to obtain correct gauge.

NOTIONS

stitch markers

scrap yarn

darning needle

sewing needle and thread

3 1¼" (3cm) buttons

GAUGE

8½ sts and 15½ rows = 4" (10cm) in St st

NOTES

YO (YARN OVER): Wrap the working yarn around the needle clockwise and knit the next st as usual. This operation creates an eyelet hole in the knitting and inc 1 st.

SK2P (SLIP 1, KNIT 2 TOGETHER, PASS SLIPPED STITCH OVER): Dec 2 sts by slipping 1 st, knitting 2 sts tog and passing the slipped st over the st rem after 2 sts were knit tog.

PM (PLACE MARKER): Slip a premade marker or a loosely knotted piece of scrap yarn in a contrasting color onto the right-hand needle after the stitch just knit to mark a spot in the knitting to refer to on future rows. When you come to a marker, simply slip it from the right-hand needle to the left-hand needle.

KFB (KNIT 1 FRONT AND BACK): Inc 1 st by knitting into the front and back of the next st.

SL MARKER OR SL ST(S) (SLIP MARKER OR SLIP STITCH[ES]): Slip a st or sts purlwise from the left needle to the right needle. When slipping a marker, knit the sts before and after it as usual.

[ ] (REPEAT OPERATION): Rep the bracketed operation the number of times indicated.

M1 (MAKE 1): Inc 1 st by picking up the bar between the next st and the st just knit and knitting into it.

K2TOG (KNIT 2 TOGETHER): Dec 1 st by knitting 2 sts tog.

FISHTAIL LACE

Work fishtail lace over a multiple of 10 sts + 11.

ROW 1 (RS): K1, *yo, k3, SK2P, k3, yo, k1; rep from * to end.

ROW 2: Purl.

ROW 3: K1, *k1, yo, k2, SK2P, k2, yo, k1, p1; rep from * to last 10 sts, k1, yo, k2, SK2P, k2, yo, k2.

ROWS 4 AND 6: P10, *k1, p9; rep from * to last st, p1.

ROW 5: K1, *k2, yo, k1, SK2P, k1, yo, k2, p1; rep from * to last 10 sts, k2, yo, k1, SK2P, k1, yo, k3.

ROW 7: K1, *k3, yo, SK2P, yo, k3, p1; rep from * to last 10 sts, k3, yo, SK2P, yo, k4.

ROW 8: Purl.

Rep Rows 1–8.

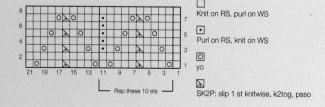

Knit on RS, purl on WS

Purl on RS, knit on WS

yo

SK2P: slip 1 st knitwise, k2tog, psso

Rep these 10 sts

YOKE

Cast on 50 (52, 52, 54, 56) sts. Do not join. Work 6 rows in garter st (knit every row), beg with a knit row.

RAGLAN SET-UP ROW (WS): K9, pm, k7 (8, 7, 7, 5), pm, k18 (18, 20, 22, 28), pm, k7 (8, 7, 7, 5), pm, k9.

RAGLAN INC ROW (RS): [Knit to 1 st before marker, KFB, sl marker, KFB] 4 times, knit to end—58 (60, 60, 62, 64) sts.

Work 1 row even.

Rep last 2 rows 8 (9, 11, 12, 13) times more—122 (132, 148, 158, 168) sts.

BODY

SEPARATE SLEEVES FROM BODY

NEXT ROW (RS): K18 (19, 21, 22, 23), place next 25 (28, 31, 33, 33) sts for first sleeve on scrap yarn to be worked later, cast on 0 (0, 2, 2, 3, 4) sts for underarm, pm for side, cast on 0 (0, 2, 2, 3, 4) sts, knit to next marker, place next 25 (28, 31, 33, 33) sts for second sleeve on scrap yarn to be worked later, cast on 0 (0, 2, 2, 3, 4) sts, pm for side, cast on 0 (0, 2, 2, 3, 4) sts, knit to end—72 (84, 94, 104, 118) sts. Do not join.

Work 1 row even.

SHAPE WAIST

WAIST INC ROW (RS): [Knit to 2 sts before marker, M1, k2, M1] twice, knit to end—76 (88, 98, 108, 122) sts.

At top, schematic diagram with measurements:

8½ (8½, 9½, 10¼, 13¼)"
(22 [22, 22, 24, 26, 34]cm)

seam trim to sleeve

12"
(31cm)

17 (19¾, 22, 24½, 27¾)"
(43 [50, 56, 62, 71]cm)

23¾ (23¾, 24¼, 24¾, 25)"
(58 [60, 62, 63, 64]cm)

seam trim to body

23½ (26¼, 28¾, 31, 34¼)"
(60 [67, 73, 79, 87]cm)

Work 1 row even.

Rep last 2 rows 6 times more—100 (112, 122, 132, 146) sts.

Work 7 rows even. Place sts on scrap yarn to be worked later.

BODY TRIM

Cast on 111 (121, 131, 141, 151) sts. Work 3 rows in garter st.

NEXT ROW (RS): Work 24 rows in fishtail lace (3 vertical patt rep). Bind off. Seam trim to live body sts, easing as necessary to fit.

SLEEVE TRIM

Cast on 31 (41, 41, 51, 51) sts. Work 3 rows in garter st.

NEXT ROW (RS): Work 32 rows in fishtail lace (4 vertical patt rep).

Bind off. Seam trim to live sleeve sts, easing as necessary to fit.

FINISHING

Seam sleeves. Seam underarms.

BUTTON BAND

With RS facing, beg just below garter st neck edge and ending just above body trim, pick up and knit approx 2 sts for every inch (or 3cm) along right front. Work 5 rows in garter st. Bind off.

BUTTONHOLE BAND

With RS facing, pick up and knit approx 2 sts for every inch (or 3cm) along left front. Work 1 row in garter st. Place 3 markers for buttonholes, evenly spaced.

NEXT ROW (RS): [Knit to marker, yo, k2tog] 3 times, knit to end. Work 3 rows in garter st. Bind off.

Weave in ends. Use a needle and thread to attach the buttons.

TEXTURIZED
TWEED COAT

In this coat, two simple stitch patterns and a gorgeous tweed yarn add up to big-time textural impact. The coat is knit from the top down in one piece; the collar and button band are picked up and knit later. While this sweater looks like a traditional tweed "professor" cardigan with its leather buttons and shawl collar, its length, belled sleeves and subtle hip shaping make it truly up to date. Pair it with a pencil skirt for the office or campus, or exchange those daytime duds for cigarette-leg pants and a beaded cami, and you're ready for a night out.

FINISHED MEASUREMENTS

BUST: 33 (37½, 43¾, 48¾, 54)" (84 [95, 111, 124, 137]cm), including front bands

YARN

7 (8, 9, 10, 11) hanks (220 yds [198m] ea) Cascade Yarns Cascade 220 Tweed (Peruvian Highland wool/Donegal blend)
COLOR CAMEL TWEED 625

NEEDLES

size US 8 (5mm) 40" (102cm) circular needle

size US 8 (5mm) 16" (40cm) circular needle

If necessary, change needle size to obtain correct gauge.

NOTIONS

stitch markers

scrap yarn or stitch holders

darning needle

7 ¾" (2cm) buttons

12 ⅝" (2cm) buttons

1 hook-and-eye clasp (optional)

GAUGE

18 sts and 28 rows = 4" (10cm) in texture patt

NOTES

PM (PLACE MARKER): Slip a premade marker or a loosely knotted piece of scrap yarn in a contrasting color onto the right-hand needle after the stitch just knit to mark a spot in the knitting to refer to on future rows. When you come to a marker, simply slip it from the right-hand needle to the left-hand needle.

[ ] (REPEAT OPERATION): Rep the bracketed operation the number of times indicated.

KFB (KNIT 1 FRONT AND BACK): Inc 1 st by knitting into the front and back of the next st.

SL MARKER OR SL ST(S) (SLIP MARKER OR SLIP STITCH[ES]): Slip a st or sts purlwise from the left needle to the right needle. When slipping a marker, knit the sts before and after it as usual.

K3TOG (KNIT 3 TOGETHER): Dec 2 sts by knitting 3 sts tog.

M1 (MAKE 1): Inc 1 st by picking up the bar between the next st and the st just knit and knitting into it.

SSK (SLIP, SLIP, KNIT): Dec 1 st by slipping 2 sts knitwise one at a time, inserting the tip of the left needle into both sts and knitting the 2 sts tog.

K2TOG (KNIT 2 TOGETHER): Dec 1 st by knitting 2 sts tog.

YO (YARN OVER): Wrap the working yarn around the needle clockwise and knit the next st as usual. This operation creates an eyelet hole in the knitting and inc 1 st.

P2TOG (PURL 2 TOGETHER): Dec 1 st by purling 2 sts tog.

WORK 2 TOG (KNIT OR PURL 2 TOGETHER): Dec 1 st by knitting or purling 2 sts tog as one, in keeping with the est patt.

LLI (LEFT LIFTED INCREASE): Inc 1 st by inserting the tip of the left needle into the back of the st 1 row below on the right needle and knitting into it.

RLI (RIGHT LIFTED INCREASE): Inc 1 st in by inserting the tip of the right needle into the back of the st 1 row below on the left needle and knitting into it to create a right-leaning increase.

TEXTURE PATTERN

Work texture patt over a multiple of 2 sts.

ROW 1 (WS): *K1, p1; rep from * to end.

ROW 2: Knit.

ROW 3: *P1, k1; rep from * to end.

ROW 4: Knit.

Rep Rows 1–4.

ALTERNATING RIB

Work alternating rib over a multiple of 4 sts.

ROW 1 (WS): *K2, p2; rep from * to end.

ROWS 2–4: Rep Row 1.

ROWS 5–8: *P2, k2; rep from * to end.

Rep Rows 1–8.

YOKE

With 40" (102cm) circular needle, cast on 52 (52, 56, 56, 60) sts. Do not join.

RAGLAN SET-UP ROW (WS): Working in texture patt, work 1 st, pm, 10 sts, pm, 30 (30, 34, 34, 38) sts, pm, 10 sts, pm, 1 st.

RAGLAN INC ROW (RS): Cont in texture patt, [work to 1 st before marker, KFB, sl marker, KFB] 4 times—60 (60, 64, 64, 68) sts.

Work 1 row even, working inc sts in texture patt.

Rep last 2 rows 9 (13, 16, 18, 21) times more—132 (164, 192, 208, 236) sts.

RAGLAN AND NECK INC ROW (RS): KFB, [work to 1 st before marker, KFB, sl marker, KFB] 4 times, work to last st, KFB—142 (174, 202, 218, 246) sts.

Work 1 row even.

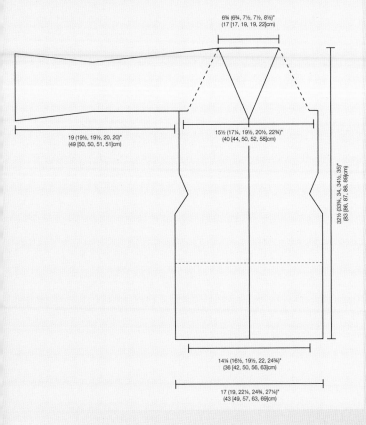

6¾ (6¾, 7½, 7½, 8½)"
(17 [17, 19, 19, 22]cm)

19 (19½, 19½, 20, 20)"
(49 [50, 50, 51, 51]cm)

15½ (17¼, 19½, 20½, 22¾)"
(40 [44, 50, 52, 58]cm)

32½ (33¾, 34, 34½, 35)"
(83 [86, 87, 88, 89]cm)

14¼ (16½, 19½, 22, 24¾)"
(36 [42, 50, 56, 63]cm)

17 (19, 22¼, 24¾, 27¼)"
(43 [49, 57, 63, 69]cm)

Rep last 2 rows 9 (9, 4, 3, 1) times more—232 (254, 242, 248, 256) sts.

Smallest sizes go on to body pattern.

SIZES 43¾ (48¾, 54)

NEXT ROW (RS): Rep Raglan and Neck Inc Row once more—252 (258, 266) sts.

NEXT ROW (WS): KFB, work to last st, KFB—254 (260, 268) sts.

Rep last 2 rows 4 (5, 7) times more—302 (320, 352) sts.

BODY

SEPARATE SLEEVES FROM BODY

ALL SIZES

NEXT ROW (RS): Work 31 (35, 43, 46, 51) sts, place next 50 (58, 64, 68, 74) sts for first sleeve on scrap yarn to be worked later, cast on 0 (0, 3, 6, 7) sts for underarm, pm for side, cast on 0 (0, 3, 6, 7) sts, work to next marker, place next 50 (58, 64, 68, 74) sts for second sleeve on scrap yarn to be worked later, cast on 0 (0, 3, 6, 7) sts, pm for side, cast on 0 (0, 3, 6, 7) sts, work to end—132 (148, 186, 208, 232) sts. Do not join.

Work 1 row even.

NECK INC ROW (RS): KFB, work to last st, KFB—134 (150, 188, 210, 234) sts.

Work 1 row even.

Rep last 2 rows 3 (5, 0, 0, 0) times—140 (160, 188, 210, 234) sts.

Work even until piece measures 7¼ (7¼, 6½, 6½, 6½)" (18 [18, 17, 17, 17]cm) from underarm, ending with a WS row.

SHAPE WAIST

WAIST DEC ROW 1 (RS): Work to marker, k3tog, work to 3 sts before next marker, k3tog, work to end—136 (156, 184, 206, 230) sts rem.

Work 9 rows even.

WAIST DEC ROW 2 (RS): Work 16 (19, 22, 25, 28) sts, pm, k3tog, work to next marker, k3tog, work to 3 sts before next marker, k3tog, work 16 (19, 22, 25, 28) sts, k3tog, pm, work to end—128 (148, 176, 198, 222) sts rem.

Work 9 rows even.

WAIST INC ROW 1 (RS): [Work to marker, M1, sl marker, k1, M1] twice, work 20 (22, 28, 31, 35) sts, M1, pm, k1, M1, work 19 (23, 27, 31, 36) sts, M1, pm, k1, M1, [work to 1 st before marker, M1, k1, sl marker, M1] twice, work to end—140 (160, 188, 210, 234) sts.

Work 9 rows even.

WAIST INC ROW 2 (RS): [Work to marker, M1, sl marker, k1, M1] 4 times, [work to 1 st before marker, M1, k1, sl marker, M1] twice, work to end—152 (172, 200, 222, 246) sts.

Work 1 row even, removing all markers.

Work even until piece measures 17 (17, 16½, 16½, 16)" (43 [43, 42, 42, 41]cm) from underarm, ending with a RS row.

NEXT ROW (WS): Work in alternating rib until piece measures 25½ (25½, 25, 25, 24½)" (65 [65, 64, 64, 62]cm) from underarm, ending with Row 3 or 7 of patt.

Bind off in patt.

SLEEVES

NEXT ROW (RS): Cast on 0 (0, 3, 6, 7) sts, cont in texture patt as est across 50 (58, 64, 68, 74) sts from scrap yarn for 1 sleeve, cast on 0 (0, 3, 6, 7) sts—50 (58, 70, 80, 88) sts. Do not join.

Work 1 row even, working cast-on sts in texture patt.

SHAPE SLEEVE

NOTE: *Smallest sizes, skip to "All Sizes"*

SIZES 43¾ (48¾, 54)

DEC ROW: SSK, work to last 2 sts, k2tog—68 (78, 86) sts rem. Work 11 (7, 4) rows even.

Rep last 12 (8, 6) rows 5 (8, 11) times more—58 (62, 64) sts rem.

ALL SIZES

Work even until piece measures 10 (10½, 10½, 11, 11)" (25 [27, 27, 28, 28]cm) from underarm, ending with a WS row.

SHAPE CUFF SLIT

NEXT ROW (RS): Work 24 (28, 28, 30, 31) sts, KFB, join a second ball of yarn, KFB, work to end—26 (30, 30, 32, 33) sts each side.

Working both sides at same time, work 11 rows even.

INC ROW (RS): First side: Work to last st, KFB; second side: KFB, work to end—27 (31, 31, 33, 34) sts each side.

Work 11 rows even.

Rep last 12 rows 3 times more—30 (34, 34, 36, 37) sts each side.

Work even until piece measures 9" (23cm) from beg of cuff, ending with Row 3 or 7 of patt. Bind off in patt.

CUFFS

LEFT CUFF BAND

With RS facing, beg at bottom left edge of left cuff slit, pick up and knit 52 sts along left edge of cuff slit. Work 3 rows in alternating rib.

BUTTONHOLE ROW (RS): Work 2 sts, [yo, p2tog, work 6 sts] 6 times, work to end.

Work 3 rows even. Bind off in patt.

RIGHT CUFF BAND

With RS facing, beg at top right edge of right cuff slit, pick up and knit 52 sts along right edge of cuff slit. Work 3 rows in alternating rib.

BUTTONHOLE ROW (RS): Work 8 sts, [yo, p2tog, work 6 sts] 5 times, yo, p2tog, work to end.

Work 3 rows even. Bind off in patt.

BUTTON BANDS

FRONT BUTTON BAND

With RS facing, beg at base of left neck shaping, pick up and knit 3 sts for every 4 rows along left front, end at top of alternating rib band with multiple of 4 sts. Work in alternating rib for 11 rows. Bind off in patt.

FRONT BUTTONHOLE BAND

With RS facing, beg at top of alternating rib band, pick up and knit 3 sts for every 4 rows along right front, end at base of right neck shaping with multiple of 4 sts. Pm for 7 buttons along the right front edge, the first 1¼" (3cm) from top, the last 1¼" (3cm) from bottom, the rem 5 evenly spaced between. Work in alternating rib for 7 rows.

BUTTONHOLE ROW (RS): [Work to marker, yo, work 2 tog] 7 times, work to end.

Work 3 rows even. Bind off in patt.

COLLAR

With RS facing, beg at base of right neck shaping, pick up and knit 52 (64, 58, 60, 66) sts along right front neck edge, 52 (52, 56, 56, 60) sts along yoke edge (1 st for every st cast on), 52 (64, 58, 60, 66) sts along left neck edge—156 (180, 172, 176, 192) sts.

Work 6 rows in k2, p2 rib. Pm at each raglan shaping point, making sure markers are placed between 2 knit or 2 purl sts.

Work 1 row alternating rib.

SHAPE CENTER OF COLLAR

SHORT ROW (RS): Cont in alternating rib as est, work to 5 sts after third marker, wrap and turn; work to 5 sts after next marker, wrap and turn; [work to 6 sts before wrap of row before previous row, wrap and turn] 4 times, work to end, working wraps tog with wrapped sts as you come to them.

Work 1 row even, working rem wraps tog with wrapped sts.

SHAPE COLLAR

ROW 1 (RS): [Work to marker, LLI, sl marker, RLI] 4 times, work to end—164 (188, 180, 184, 200) sts.

ROW 2: Work even, working inc sts in alternating rib.

ROW 3: Rep Row 1—172 (196, 188, 192, 208) sts.

ROWS 4–12: Work even.

ROW 13: Rep Row 1—180 (204, 196, 200, 216) sts.

ROW 14: Work even.

ROW 15: Rep Row 1—188 (212, 204, 208, 224) sts.

ROWS 16–28: Work even.

ROW 29: Rep Row 1—196 (220, 212, 216, 232) sts.

ROW 30: Work even.

ROW 31: Rep Row 1—204 (228, 220, 224, 240) sts.

ROWS 32–43: Work even.

Bind off in patt.

FINISHING

Seam sleeves.

Seam the edges of the cuff bands to the sleeves. Seam the underarms. Attach the buttons. Attach a hook-and-eye clasp (optional) to the top of the front bands.

Weave in ends.

PUFF-SLEEVED
HOODIE

This hoodie is knit from pure, hand-dyed merino wool. Each piece is knit separately and then seamed together at the end. The cloudlike appearance of the resulting fabric is mirrored in its soft, cozy feel. This will quickly become your "go-to" sweater. It combines the look of the traditional cardigan with puffy Victorian sleeves and a nice, roomy hood for an updated look. This cardigan looks equally great dressed up over a tweed skirt or with jeans and a tee on the weekend.

FINISHED MEASUREMENTS

BUST: 36 (39½, 44½, 49½, 56½)" (91 [100, 113, 126, 144]cm)

YARN

8 (9, 10, 11, 12) hanks (215 yds [194m] ea) Malabrigo Merino Worsted (100% merino wool)
   COLOR BLUE SURF

NEEDLES

size US 7 (4.5mm) straight needles

size US 8 (5mm) straight needles

If necessary, change needle size to obtain correct gauge.

NOTIONS

3 1¾" (5cm) wide toggles

3 1⅜" (3cm) wide toggles

darning needle

GAUGE

19 sts and 27 rows = 4" (10cm) in St st, using larger needles

NOTES

SSK (SLIP, SLIP, KNIT): Dec 1 st by slipping 2 sts knitwise one at a time, inserting the tip of the left needle into both sts and knitting the 2 sts tog.

K2TOG (KNIT 2 TOGETHER): Dec 1 st by knitting 2 sts tog.

P2TOG (PURL 2 TOGETHER): Dec 1 st by purling 2 sts tog.

SEED STITCH

Work seed st over a multiple of 2 sts.

ROW 1 (WS): *P1, k1; rep from * to end.

ROW 2: *K1, p1; rep from * to end.

Rep Rows 1–2.

BACK

With larger needles, cast on 86 (94, 106, 118; 134) sts. Work in seed st until piece measures 3½" (9cm) from beg, ending with a WS row.

NEXT ROW (RS): Work in St st until piece measures 12 (12½, 13, 13½, 14)" (30 [32, 33, 34, 36]cm) from beg, ending with a WS row.

Purl 1 row, knit 1 row, purl 2 rows, knit 2 rows, purl 1 row, knit 1 row.

NEXT ROW (RS): K3, *p2, k2; rep from * to last 3 sts, p3.

Rep last row for 3½" (9cm), ending with a WS row.

Purl 1 row, knit 1 row, purl 2 rows, knit 2 rows, purl 1 row, knit 1 row.

NEXT ROW (RS): Work in St st until piece measures 20½ (21, 21½, 22, 22½)" (52 [53, 55, 56, 57]cm) from beg, ending with a WS row.

SHAPE ARMHOLES

NEXT ROW (RS): Bind off 3 (4, 5, 8, 12) sts at beg of next 2 rows—80 (86, 96, 102, 110) sts rem.

DEC ROW (RS): K1, SSK, work to last 3 sts, k2tog, k1—78 (84, 94, 100, 108) sts rem.

Work 1 row even.

Rep last 2 rows 7 (9, 11, 11, 12) times more—64 (66, 72, 78, 84) sts rem.

Work even until armhole measures 7 (7½, 8, 8½, 9)" (18 [19, 20, 22, 23]cm) from beg of shaping, ending with a WS row.

SHAPE SHOULDERS AND NECK

NEXT ROW (RS): Bind off 7 (8, 8, 10, 11) sts, work 10 (10, 11, 12, 14) sts, join a second ball of yarn, bind off center 30 (30, 34, 34, 34) sts, work to end.

NEXT ROW (WS): Left side: Bind off 7 (8, 8, 10, 11) sts, work to end; right side: Bind off 2 sts, work to end.

NEXT ROW (RS): Right side: Bind off 8 (8, 9, 10, 12) sts; left side: BO 2 sts, work to end.

NEXT ROW (WS): Left side: Bind off.

RIGHT FRONT

With larger needles, cast on 38 (42, 50, 54, 62) sts. Work in seed st until piece measures 3½" (9cm) from beg, ending with a WS row.

Purl 1 row, knit 1 row, purl 2 rows, knit 2 rows, purl 1 row, knit 1 row.

NEXT ROW (RS): K3, *p2, k2; rep from * to last 3 sts, p3.

Rep last row for 3½" (9cm), ending with a WS row.

Purl 1 row, knit 1 row, purl 2 rows, knit 2 rows, purl 1 row, knit 1 row.

NEXT ROW (RS): Work in St st until piece measures 20½ (21, 21½, 22, 22½)" (52 [53, 55, 56, 57]cm) from beg, ending with a RS row.

SHAPE ARMHOLE

NEXT ROW (WS): Bind off 3 (4, 5, 8, 12) sts, work to end—35 (38, 45, 46, 50) sts rem.

NEXT ROW (RS): Work to last 3 sts, k2tog, k1—34 (37, 44, 45, 49) sts rem.

Work 1 row even.

Rep last 2 rows 7 (9, 11, 11, 12) times more—27 (28, 33, 34, 37) sts rem.

Work even until armhole measures 7 (7½, 8, 8½, 9)" (18 [19, 20, 22, 23]cm) from beg of shaping, ending with a RS row.

SHAPE SHOULDERS

NEXT ROW (WS): Bind off 7 (8, 8, 10, 11) sts, work to end—20 (20, 25, 24, 26) sts rem.

Work 1 row even.

NEXT ROW (WS): Bind off 8 (8, 9, 10, 12) sts, work to end—12 (12, 16, 14, 14) sts rem.

Work 1 row even. Bind off.

LEFT FRONT

Work as for right front, reversing shaping, and working SSK instead of k2tog.

SLEEVES

With larger needles, cast on 86 (86, 90, 90, 90) sts. Work in seed st until piece measures 4" (10cm) from beg, ending with a WS row.

SHAPE SLEEVE

DEC ROW (RS): Working in St st, k1, SSK, work to last 3 sts, k2tog, k1—84 (84, 88, 88, 88) sts rem.

Work 3 (5, 5, 11, 37) rows even.

Rep last 4 (6, 6, 12, 38) rows 8 (11, 4, 2, 1) times more—68 (62, 80, 84, 86) sts rem.

SIZES 36 (44½, 49½)

Rep Dec Row once more—66 (78, 82) sts rem.

Work 5 (7, 13) rows even.

Rep last 6 (8, 14) rows 4 (4, 1) times more—58 (70, 80) sts rem.

Rep Dec Row once more—56 (68, 78) sts rem.

Work 1 row even.

ALL SIZES

Work even until piece measures 16 (16, 17, 17, 17)" (41 [41, 43, 43, 43]cm) from beg, ending with a WS row.

SHAPE CAP

NEXT ROW (RS): Bind off 3 (4, 5, 8, 12) sts at beg of next 2 rows—50 (54, 58, 62, 62) sts rem.

Work even until piece measures 5 (5½, 6, 6½, 7)" (13 (14, 15, 17, 18]cm) from beg of cap shaping, ending with a WS row.

DEC ROW (RS): K1, SSK, work to last 3 sts, k2tog, k1—48 (52, 56, 60, 60) sts rem.

Work 1 row even.

Rep last 2 rows 4 times more—40 (44, 48, 52, 52) sts rem.

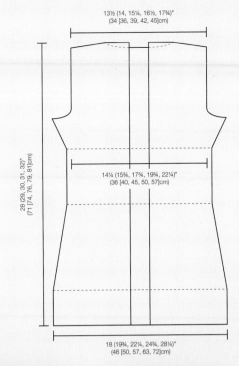

13½ (14, 15¼, 16½, 17¾)"
(34 [36, 39, 42, 45]cm)

28 (29, 30, 31, 32)"
(71 [74, 76, 79, 81]cm)

14¼ (15¾, 17¾, 19¾, 22¼)"
(36 [40, 45, 50, 57]cm)

18 (19¾, 22¼, 24¾, 28¼)"
(46 [50, 57, 63, 72]cm)

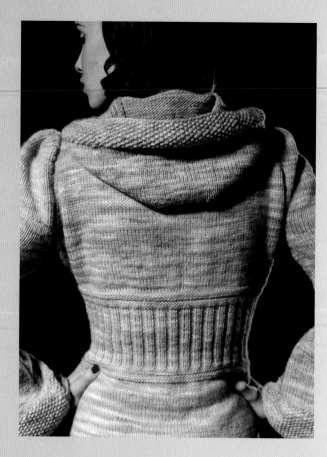

NEXT ROW (RS): *K2tog; rep from * to end—20 (22, 24, 26, 26) sts rem.

NEXT ROW (WS): *P2tog; rep from * to end—10 (11, 12, 13, 13) sts rem. Bind off.

HOOD

With larger needles, CO 110 (112, 114, 116, 118) sts. Work 8 rows in seed st. Work 6 rows in St st.

SHAPE HOOD

DEC ROW (RS): K1, SSK, work to last 3 sts, k2tog, k1—108 (110, 112, 114, 116) sts rem.

Work 7 rows even.

Rep last 8 rows 4 times more—100 (102, 104, 106, 108) sts rem.

Work even until piece measures 5 (5, 5¾, 5½, 5½)" (13 [13, 15, 14, 14]cm) from beg, ending with a WS row.

NEXT ROW (RS): Bind off 34 (35, 36, 37, 38) sts at beg of next 2 rows—32 sts rem.

Work even until piece measures 7¼ (7¼, 7½, 7¾, 8)" (18 [18, 19, 20, 20]cm) from bind-off row, ending with a WS row. Bind off. Seam straight edges of center section to bound-off edges of side sections.

FINISHING

Seam shoulders. Set in sleeves. Seam sides and sleeves.

FRONT BANDS

With RS facing and using smaller needle, pick up and knit approx 3 sts for every 4 rows along right front edge, ending with an even number of sts. Work 8 rows in seed st. Bind off in patt. Rep for left front band.

Sew the bottom of the hood along the neck edge with yarn and a darning needle. Attach toggles evenly spaced along both fronts, with the larger toggles on top and the smaller toggles on bottom.

Weave in ends.

12¼ (12¼, 13¼, 13¼, 13½)"
(31 [31, 34, 34, 34]cm)

22¾ (23¼, 24¾, 25¼, 25¾)"
(58 [59, 63, 64, 66]cm)

seam to neck edge

seam to center section

seam to bound-off edge

seam to neck edge

face edge

23¼ (23½, 24, 24¼, 24¾)"
(59 [60, 61, 62, 63]cm)

6¾"
(17cm)

20¼ (20½, 21¼, 21¼, 21¼)"
(52 [52, 54, 54, 54]cm)

11¾ (13, 14¼, 16½, 18)"
(30 [33, 36, 42, 46]cm)

FULL-LENGTH
TOGGLE COAT

This coat is big on texture and simple to knit. Knit from the neckline to the hem in one piece, the coat incorporates bust and hip shaping. All the lace details are created with simple paired increases and decreases. The front edges are faced with satin ribbon for stability, and the closures are jewelry toggles found in the beading section of your local craft store. Choose any style and size of toggle you like, or substitute buttons or hooks and eyes if you choose.

FINISHED MEASUREMENTS

BUST (CLOSED), UNSTRETCHED: 24½ (28¾, 32¾, 37)" (62 [73, 83, 94]cm)

BUST (CLOSED), STRETCHED: 32 (37½, 43, 48½)" (81 [95, 109, 123]cm)

YARN

10 (12, 14, 17) hanks (65 yds [59m] ea) Malabrigo Aquarella (100% wool)
    COLOR 16 INDY

NOTE: *As this garment must stretch significantly to fit across the bust, be sure to use a yarn that gives and stretches.*

NEEDLES

size US 13 (9 mm) 29" (74cm) circular needle

If necessary, change needle size to obtain correct gauge.

NOTIONS

stitch markers

stitch holders or scrap yarn

darning needle

sewing needle

sewing thread to match ribbon

12 toggle closures (found in bead section of hobby shop)

5½' (2m) 1½" (4cm) wide ribbon for front facings

GAUGE

9½ sts and 11 rows = 4" (10cm) in St st, unstretched

7¼ sts and 12 rows = 4" (10cm) in St st, stretched

NOTES

PM (PLACE MARKER): Slip a premade marker or a loosely knotted piece of scrap yarn in a contrasting color onto the right-hand needle after the stitch just knit to mark a spot in the knitting to refer to on future rows. When you come to a marker, simply slip it from the right-hand needle to the left-hand needle.

KFB (KNIT 1 FRONT AND BACK): Inc 1 st by knitting into the front and back of the next st.

[ ] (REPEAT OPERATION): Rep the bracketed operation the number of times indicated.

SL MARKER OR SL ST(S) (SLIP MARKER OR SLIP STITCH[ES]): Slip a st or sts purlwise from the left needle to the right needle. When slipping a marker, knit the sts before and after it as usual.

SSK (SLIP, SLIP, KNIT): Dec 1 st by slipping 2 sts knitwise one at a time, inserting the tip of the left needle into both sts and knitting the 2 sts tog.

K2TOG (KNIT 2 TOGETHER): Dec 1 st by knitting 2 sts tog.

YO (YARN OVER): Wrap the working yarn around the needle clockwise and knit the next st as usual. This operation creates an eyelet hole in the knitting and inc 1 st.

SEED STITCH

Work seed st over a multiple of 2 sts.

ALL ROWS: *K1, p1; rep from * to end.

YOKE

Cast on 16 (20, 24, 28) sts.

ROW 1 (WS): P4 (5, 6, 7), pm, p8 (10, 12, 14), pm, p4 (5, 6, 7).

ROW 2: KFB, [knit to 1 st before marker, KFB, sl marker, KFB] twice, knit to last st, KFB—22 (26, 30, 34) sts.

ROW 3 AND ALL ODD ROWS (WS): Purl.

ROWS 4–9 (11, 13, 15): Rep Rows 2–3—40 (50, 60, 70) sts.

ROW 10 (12, 14, 16): Rep Row 2—46 (56, 66, 76) sts.

ROW 12 (14, 16, 18): Cast on 1 st using Knitting-On method (see page 138 of the Special Techniques Glossary), KFB, pm, KFB, [knit to 1 st before marker, KFB, sl marker, KFB] twice, knit to last st, KFB, pm, cast on 1 st using Backward-Loop method (see page 138 of the Special Techniques Glossary), sl st to left needle, twisting st as you sl it, KFB—56 (66, 76, 86) sts.

ROW 14 (16, 18, 20): [KFB] twice, sl marker, KFB, [knit to 1 st before marker, KFB, pm, KFB] 3 times, KFB—66 (76, 86, 96) sts.

ROW 16 (18, 20, 22): KFB, [knit to 1 st before marker, KFB, sl marker, KFB] 4 times, knit to last st, KFB—76 (86, 96, 106) sts.

ROW 17 (19, 21, 23): Purl.

ROWS 18 (20, 22, 24)–19 (23, 27, 31): Rep Rows 16 (18, 20, 22) and 17 (19, 21, 23)—86 (106, 126, 146) sts.

ROW 20 (24, 28, 32): Cast on 6 sts using Knitting-On method, [knit to 1 st before marker, KFB, sl marker, KFB] 4 times, knit to end—100 (120, 140, 160) sts.

ROW 21 (25, 29, 33): Cast on 6 sts using Knitting-On method, purl to end—106 (126, 146, 166) sts.

SEPARATE SLEEVES FROM BODY

ROW 22 (26, 30, 34) (RS): P15 (17, 19, 21), place next 24 (29, 34, 39) sts for first sleeve on scrap yarn to be worked later, p28 (34, 40, 46), place next 24 (29, 34, 39) sts for second sleeve on scrap yarn to be worked later, p15 (17, 19, 21)—58 (68, 78, 88) sts on needle.

BODY

ROWS 23 (27, 31, 35)–37 (41, 45, 49): Work even in St st, beg with a purl row.

ROW 38 (42, 46, 50): K1 (0, 1, 0), *SSK, k2tog, [yo] twice; rep from * to last 5 (4, 5, 4) sts, SSK, k2tog, k1 (0, 1, 0)—56 (66, 76, 86) sts rem.

ROW 39 (43, 47, 51) AND FOLL ODD ROWS (WS): P3 (2, 3, 2), *k1, p1 (into double yo), p2; rep from * to last 1 (0, 1, 0) sts, p1 (0, 1, 0).

ROW 40 (44, 48, 52): K2 (1, 2, 1), *k2tog, [yo] twice, SSK; rep from * to last 2 (1, 2, 1) st(s), k2 (1, 2, 1).

ROW 42 (46, 50, 54): Rep Row 40 (44, 48, 52).

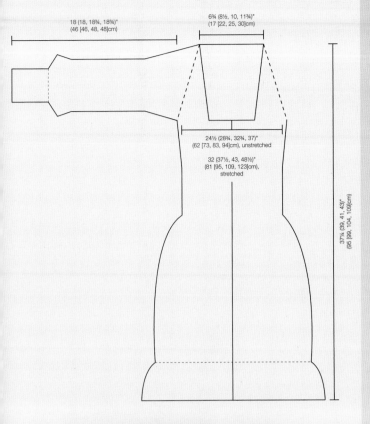

18 (18, 18¾, 18¾)"
(46 [46, 48, 48]cm)

6¾ (8½, 10, 11¾)"
(17 [22, 25, 30]cm)

24½ (28¾, 32¾, 37)"
(62 [73, 83, 94]cm), unstretched

32 (37½, 43, 48½)"
(81 [95, 109, 123]cm),
stretched

37¼ (39, 41, 43)"
(95 [99, 104, 109]cm)

ROW 44 (48, 52, 56): K2 (1, 2, 1), *SSK, k2tog, [yo] twice; rep from * to last 6 (5, 6, 5) st, SSK, k2tog, k2 (1, 2, 1)—54 (64, 74, 84) sts rem.

ROW 45 (49, 53, 57): P4 (3, 4, 3), *k1, p1 (into double yo), p2; rep from * to last 4 (3, 4, 3) sts, k4 (3, 4, 3).

ROW 46 (50, 54, 58): K5 (4, 5, 4), *[yo] twice, k4; rep from * to last 1 (0, 1, 0) st, k1 (0, 1, 0)—78 (94, 108, 124) sts.

Work even until body measures 21½ (22, 22½, 23)" (55 [56, 57, 58]cm) from underarm, ending with a WS row.

HEMLINE TRIM

ROWS 1, 3 AND 5 (RS): K1 (1, 0, 0), *k2tog, [yo] twice, SSK; rep from * to last 1 (1, 0, 0) st, k1 (1, 0, 0).

ROWS 2, 4 AND 6: P2 (2, 1, 1), *k1, p1 (into double yo), p2; rep from * to last 4 (4, 3, 3) sts, k1, p1 (into double yo), p2 (2, 1, 1).

ROW 7: K3 (3, 2, 2), *k2tog, [yo] twice, SSK; rep from * to last 3 (3, 2, 2) sts, k3 (3, 2, 2).

ROW 8: P4 (4, 3, 3), *k1, p1 (into double yo, p2; rep from * to last 6 (6, 5, 5) sts, k1, p1 (into double yo), p4 (4, 3, 3).

ROW 9: K5 (5, 6, 6), *yo, k4; rep from * to last 1 (1, 2, 2) st(s), k1 (1, 2, 2)—96 (116, 133, 153) sts.

Work 3 rows St st, beg with a knit row, dec 0 (0, 1, 1) st on last row—96 (116, 132, 152) sts rem.

Work 13 rows of seed st. Bind off.

SLEEVES

Replace 24 (29, 34, 39) held sts of one sleeve on needle. Do not join.

ROW 1 (RS): K0 (0, 1, 1), *SSK, k2tog, [yo] twice; rep from * to last 4 (5, 5, 6) sts, SSK, k2tog, k0 (1, 1, 2)—22 (27, 32, 37) sts rem.

SIZES 32 AND 43 (STRETCHED)

ROW 2: P2 (3), *k1, p1 (into double yo), p2; rep from * to last 0 (1) st, k0 (1).

SIZES 37½ AND 48½ (STRETCHED)

ROW 2: P2tog, p1 (2), *k1, p1 (into double yo), p2; rep from * to last 0 (1) st, k0 (1)—26 (36) sts rem.

ALL SIZES

ROWS 3 AND 5: K1 (1, 2, 2), *k2tog, [yo] twice, SSK; rep from * to last 1 (1, 2, 2) sts, k1 (1, 2, 2).

ROWS 4 AND 6: P2 (2, 3, 3), *k1, p1 (into double yo), p2; rep from * to last 4 (4, 5, 5) sts, k1, p1 (into double yo), p2 (2, 3, 3).

ROW 7: K3 (3, 4, 4), *k2tog, [yo] twice, SSK; rep from * to last 3 (3, 4, 4) sts, k3 (3, 4, 4).

ROW 8: P4 (4, 5, 5), *k1, p1 (into double yo), p2; rep from * to last 2 (2, 3, 3) sts, p2 (2, 3, 3).

ROW 9: K5 (5, 6, 6), *yo, k4; rep from * to last 1 (1, 2, 2) st(s), k1 (1, 2, 2)—26 (31, 38, 43) sts.

ROWS 10–30 (30, 34, 34): Work even in St st.

SIZES 32 AND 43 (STRETCHED)

ROW 31 (35): K1, *k2tog, [yo] twice, SSK; rep from * to last st, k1.

SIZES 37½ AND 48½ (STRETCHED)

ROW 31 (35): SSK, *k2tog, [yo] twice, SSK; rep from * to last st, k1—30 (42) sts rem.

ALL SIZES

ROW 32 (32, 36, 36) AND FOLL EVEN ROWS: P2, *k1, p1 (into double yo), p2; rep from * to end.

ROWS 33 (33, 37, 37) AND 35 (35, 39, 39): K1, *k2tog, [yo] twice, SSK; rep from * to last st, k1.

SIZES 32 AND 37½ (STRETCHED)

ROW 37: K3, *yo, k4; rep from * to last 3 sts, k3—32 (37) sts.

ROW 38: Purl.

ALL SIZES

ROWS 39 (39, 41, 41) AND 40 (40, 42, 42): Work even in St st.

ROW 41 (41, 43, 43): K1 (1, 1, 0), [SSK, k1] 5 (6, 6, 7) times, [k2tog, k1] 5 (6, 6, 7) times, k1 (0, 1, 0)—22 (25, 26, 28) sts rem.

Work 17 rows in seed st. Bind off.

COLLAR

With RS facing, beg at right sleeve, pick up and knit 1 st for every st around neck, ending at left sleeve. Adjust the number of sts if necessary to achieve a multiple of 2 sts.

Work 15 rows of seed st, work k2tog at beg and SSK at end of every RS row.

Bind off.

FINISHING

Cut 2 lengths of ribbon to match the length of the front from the cast-on sts at the neck edge to the bound-off sts at the bottom edge, plus 1" (3cm) for finishing the edges. Fold the top and bottom edges over ½" (1cm). Using a sewing needle and thread, sew the ribbon along the WS of each front edge.

Note: Cut ribbon to fit around eyelets so it doesn't show on RS.

Sew the toggle closures evenly spaced along the front edges, beg 1" (3cm) below the neck edge and ending just above the seed st border at the bottom.

Seam sleeves. Weave in ends. Block if desired.

SHORT-AND-SWEET
COAT

How indulgent is it to knit a coat from pure bulky alpaca? Nothing makes you feel more special than knitting something you love out of a yarn that blows your mind! This coat is knit in one piece from the neckline to the hem, and the sleeves can either be worked flat and seamed or knit in the round on double-pointed needles. I embellished my coat with a brightly dyed ribbon yarn and big gold buttons. The three-quarter sleeves and slightly flared body give this coat a mod feel.

FINISHED MEASUREMENTS

BUST: 34 (40½, 47, 53½)" (86 [103, 119, 136]cm)

YARN

11 (13, 14, 16) hanks (45 yds [41m] ea) Blue Sky Alpacas Bulky Naturals (alpaca/wool blend)
    COLOR 1008 BLACK BEAR

NEEDLES

size US 15 (10mm) 40" (102cm) circular needle

If necessary, change needle size to obtain correct gauge.

NOTIONS

stitch markers

scrap yarn

darning needle

sewing needle and thread to match ribbon

8 1" (3cm) buttons

approx 6 yds (5.5m) ¼" (6mm) ribbon for trim

1¾ yds (1.5m) 1" (3cm) ribbon for button band facing

GAUGE

7½ sts and 11 rows = 4" (10cm) in St st

NOTES

PM (PLACE MARKER): Slip a premade marker or a loosely knotted piece of scrap yarn in a contrasting color onto the right-hand needle after the stitch just knit to mark a spot in the knitting to refer to on future rows. When you come to a marker, simply slip it from the right-hand needle to the left-hand needle.

[ ] (REPEAT OPERATION): Rep the bracketed operation the number of times indicated.

KFB (KNIT 1 FRONT AND BACK): Inc 1 st by knitting into the front and back of the next st.

SL MARKER OR SL ST(S) (SLIP MARKER OR SLIP STITCH[ES]): Slip a st or sts purlwise from the left needle to the right needle. When slipping a marker, knit the sts before and after it as usual.

M1 (MAKE 1): Inc 1 st by picking up the bar between the next st and the st just knit and knitting into it.

SSK (SLIP, SLIP, KNIT): Dec 1 st by slipping 2 sts knitwise one at a time, inserting the tip of the left needle into both sts and knitting the 2 sts tog.

K2TOG (KNIT 2 TOGETHER): Dec 1 st by knitting 2 sts tog.

YOKE

Cast on 60 sts. Do not join.

RAGLAN SET-UP ROW (WS): [K10, pm] twice, k20, [pm, k10] twice.

Knit 2 rows.

RAGLAN INC ROW (RS): [Knit to 1 st before marker, KFB, sl marker, KFB] 4 times, knit to end—68 sts.

Purl 1 row.

Rep last 2 rows 5 (7, 8, 9) times more—108 (124, 132, 140) sts.

BODY

SEPARATE SLEEVES FROM BODY

NEXT ROW (RS): K16 (18, 19, 20), place next 22 (26, 28, 30) sts for first sleeve on scrap yarn to be worked later, cast on 0 (1, 3, 5) sts for underarm, pm, cast on 0 (1, 3, 5) sts, knit to next marker, place next 22 (26, 28, 30) sts for second sleeve on scrap yarn to be worked later, cast on 0 (1, 3, 5) sts, pm, cast on 0 (1, 3, 5) sts, k16 (18, 19, 20)—64 (76, 88, 100) sts. Do not join.

Work 1 row even.

BODY INC ROW 1 (RS): [Knit to 1 st before marker, KFB, sl marker, KFB] twice, knit to end—68 (80, 92, 104) sts.

Work 3 rows even.

Rep last 4 rows once more—72 (84, 96, 108) sts.

Work even until piece measures 12 (13, 14, 15)" (31 [33, 36, 38]cm) from underarm, ending with a WS row.

BODY INC ROW 2 (RS): K2 (4, 2, 4), M1, [k3 (0, 4, 0), M1] 2 (0, 2, 0) times, [k4 (4, 5, 5), M1] 14 (19, 15, 20) times, [k3 (0, 4, 0), M1] 2 (0, 2, 0) times, k2 (4, 3, 4)—91 (104, 116, 129) sts.

Work even until piece measures 18" (46cm) from underarm, ending with a RS row. Knit 1 row. Bind off knitwise.

SLEEVES

NEXT ROW (RS): Cast on 0 (1, 3, 5) sts, k22 (26, 28, 30) sts from scrap yarn for 1 sleeve, cast on 0 (1, 3, 5) sts—22 (28, 34, 40) sts. Purl 1 row.

SIZES 34 (40½)

SHAPE SLEEVE

INC ROW (RS): KFB, knit to last st, KFB—24 (30) sts.

Work 3 (9) rows even.

Rep last 4 (10) rows 4 (1) times—32 sts.

Rep Inc Row once more—34 sts.

SIZES 47 AND 53½

SHAPE SLEEVE

DEC ROW (RS): SSK, knit to last 2 sts, k2tog—38 sts rem.

Work 9 rows even.

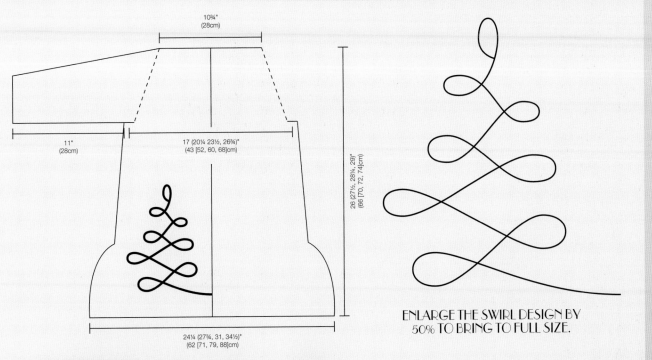

10¾"
(28cm)

11"
(28cm)

17 (20¼ 23½, 26¾)"
(43 [52, 60, 68]cm)

26 (27½, 28¼, 29)"
(66 [70, 72, 74]cm)

24¼ (27¾, 31, 34½)"
(62 [71, 79, 88]cm)

ENLARGE THE SWIRL DESIGN BY
50% TO BRING TO FULL SIZE.

Rep last 10 rows once more—36 sts rem.

Rep Dec Row once more—34 sts rem.

ALL SIZES

Work even until piece measures 10" (25cm) from under-arm, ending with a RS row. Knit 2 rows. Bind off purlwise.

FINISHING

Seam sleeves. Seam underarms.

Attach 8 buttons evenly spaced along the left front. Using a single strand of yarn and a darning needle, work 8 button loops along the right front, opposite the buttons. Work each loop by running a strand of yarn from the WS to the RS and then back to the WS a few rows below where the yarn came up, leaving just enough room to fit a button through the loop. Tie the ends of the loop, making sure the loop lies flat on RS and does not bunch the fabric.

Weave in ends.

Stitch ¼" (6mm) wide ribbon around the neckline, cuffs and hem, and on the right front, following the patt on this page, with a sewing needle and thread to match the ribbon. Stitch 1" (3cm) wide ribbon on the WS along the inside front edges.

FINISHING TOUCH
ACCESSORIES, HANDBAGS AND CLUTCHES

The projects in this chapter add just the right touch of glam to any outfit. While all these projects are big on texture, some can be knit in an afternoon (such as the *Fur Collar* on page 122), while others will take a bit longer (see the *Lace Sleeves* on page 126). Finishing off your outfit with one of these glam accents will pull your whole look together and make you feel like a million bucks.

NOTES

KFB (KNIT 1 FRONT AND BACK): Inc 1 st by knitting into the front and back of the next st.

FINISHED MEASUREMENTS

22" × 5" (56cm × 13cm), not including ribbon

YARN

1 ball (100 yds [90m]) Cascade Yarns Fixation (cotton/elastic blend)
   COLOR 8990 BLACK (A)
1 ball (8.5 yds [8m]) Fur Yarn by Paula Lishman in Fox
   COLOR DENIM (B)

NEEDLES

size US 11 (8mm) straight needles

NOTIONS

7' (2.25m) 1" (3cm) wide satin ribbon

sewing needle and black sewing thread

GAUGE

8 sts = 4" (10cm) in garter st

FUR COLLAR

Fur collars were big in the fashion world a few years ago, and I just loved that trend! It's one that stuck with me, even though I'm not a big fur person. This fur yarn is manufactured by a company that ensures the source of the fur is well regulated and environmentally sustainable. The fur also accounts for the livelihood of a certain segment of the Canadian population. The collar is knit using a combination of fur yarn and cotton yarn, so you actually use less yardage than you think you would. After knitting the collar, use a brush to fluff up the fur, and you can't even tell it was knit!

COLLAR

Using yarn A, cast on 44 sts.

ROWS 1–2: Change to yarn B. Knit.

ROWS 3 AND 5: Change to yarn A. Knit.

ROW 4: KFB, knit to last st, KFB—46 sts.

ROWS 6–20: Rep Rows 1–5.

ROWS 21–22: Rep Rows 1–2.

Change to yarn A. Bind off. Weave in ends.

FINISHING

Cut the ribbon into 2 equal pieces. Using a sewing needle and thread, sew the narrow end of each piece of ribbon to the side (short) edge of the collar, in line with the cast-on edge of the collar.

LACY
ACCENT SCARF

This scarf is knit using a simple two-row lace pattern, and it looks equally great from the front or from the back…there's no *wrong side* to this project! I've chosen a fine-gauge wool-and-silk-blend yarn for this project, but it looks equally great knit in a worsted weight or even a bulky yarn.

FINISHED MEASUREMENTS

6½" × 72" (17 × 183cm)

YARN

1 ball (630 yds [567m] ea) Jagger Spun Zephyr Wool-Silk (merino wool/Chinese tussah silk blend)
COLOR TEAL

NEEDLES

size US 6 (4mm) straight needles
If necessary, change needle size to obtain correct gauge.

GAUGE

31 sts and 20 rows = 4" (10cm) in lace patt

NOTES

YO (YARN OVER): Wrap the working yarn around the needle clockwise, and knit the next st as usual. This operation creates an eyelet hole in the knitting and inc 1 st.

P2TOG (PURL 2 TOGETHER): Dec 1 st by purling 2 sts tog.

LACE PATTERN

Work lace patt over a multiple of 7 sts +1.

ROW 1: K1, *p1, k1, yo, p2tog, k1, p1, k1; rep from * to end.

ROW 2: P1, *k2, yo, p2tog, k2, p1; rep from * to end.

Rep Rows 1–2.

SCARF

Cast on 50 sts. Work in lace patt until piece measures 72" (183cm). Bind off.

FINISHING

Weave in ends. Block lightly.

LACE SLEEVES

In this flowing accessory, I'm playing with scale. I love lace knit on big needles, and this rayon-metallic-blend yarn really gleams. The sleeves are knit as two rectangles, and then they're joined at the back and edged in a length of garter stitch. This garment looks great over a black camisole with long black pants and heels, but it also works for daytime paired with jeans and cowboy boots.

FINISHED MEASUREMENTS

CUFF TO CUFF: 56" (142cm)

YARN

7 balls (113 yds [102m] ea) Muench Yarns Verikeri (nylon/16% polyester blend)
   COLOR 4103

NOTE: *Be sure to purchase additional yarn if you add length to the pieces.*

NEEDLES

size US 11 (8mm) straight needles

2 size US 10 (6mm) double-pointed needles (dpn)

If necessary, change needle size to obtain correct gauge.

NOTIONS

darning needle

T pins

GAUGE

13 sts and 14 rows = 4" (10cm) in foaming-waves patt, using larger needles, unstretched

NOTES

K2TOG (KNIT 2 TOGETHER): Dec 1 st by knitting 2 sts tog.

YO (YARN OVER): Wrap the working yarn around the needle clockwise and knit the next st as usual. This operation creates an eyelet hole in the knitting and inc 1 st.

[ ] (REPEAT OPERATION): Rep the bracketed operation the number of times indicated.

SKP (SLIP 1, KNIT 1, PASS SLIPPED STITCH OVER): Dec 1 st by passing the first sl st over the knit st.

FOAMING-WAVES PATTERN

Work foaming-waves patt over a multiple of 12 sts + 1.

ROW 1 (RS): Knit.

ROWS 2–4: Knit.

ROW 5: K1, *[k2tog] twice, [yo, k1] 3 times, yo, [SKP] twice, k1; rep from * to end.

ROW 6: Purl.

ROWS 7–12: Rep Rows 5–6.

Rep Rows 1–12.

NOTE: *This pattern is easily customizable. If you want shorter or longer sleeves, work each back/sleeve piece until it is the desired length from the center back to where you want the sleeve to end, keeping in mind that the fabric will stretch significantly.*

To adjust the fit around the back and shoulders, work the edging band until it fits comfortably around your back and shoulders, stretching it to fit. Because the edging band is worked in garter st, it will have considerable stretch. Be sure the edging band is not too loose, or the shrug will not stay on your shoulders.

Note that if you add length to either of the pieces, you may need additional yarn to complete the project.

BACK/SLEEVE (MAKE 2)

With larger needles, cast on 97 sts. Work in foaming waves patt for 28" (71cm), or to desired length from center back to end of piece, ending with a WS row. Bind off.

EDGING BAND

With dpn and yarn doubled, cast on 11 sts. Work in garter st (knit every row) until piece measures 40" (102cm) or until piece fits comfortably around back and shoulders, slightly stretched, as for a shrug. Bind off.

FINISHING

Seam the bound-off edges of the back/sleeve pieces together. Seam the cast-on and bound-off edges of the edging band together. Fold the back/sleeve piece in half widthwise, with the seam at the center and the cast-on edges at the outside edges; lay it on a flat surface. Lay the edging band flat at the open edge of the back/sleeve piece, with the edging band seam lined up with the back/sleeve piece seam; pin it to the back/sleeve piece. Seam the edging band to the back/sleeve piece. Seam the back/sleeve piece from the cast-on edges to the edging band.

Weave in ends.

OPENWORK
HANDBAG

This is another quick-and-easy project. The lace is a simple yarn-over, knit-two-together pattern, and it works up very fast. The body of the purse is then sewn to a cloth rectangle, and then the handles are added. I've chosen a textural yarn, but this would also work with yarns as varied as chenille, linen or even bulky wool. Let your imagination run wild!

NOTES

[ ] (REPEAT OPERATION): Rep the bracketed operation the number of times indicated.

K2TOG (KNIT 2 TOGETHER): Dec 1 st by knitting 2 sts tog.

YO (YARN OVER): Wrap the working yarn around the needle clockwise, and knit the next st as usual. This operation creates an eyelet hole in the knitting and inc 1 st.

SSK (SLIP, SLIP, KNIT): Dec 1 st by slipping 2 sts knitwise one at a time, inserting the tip of the left needle into both sts and knitting the 2 sts tog.

LACE PATTERN

Work lace patt over a multiple of 10 sts + 7.

ROWS 1, 3, 5 AND 7 (RS): K2, [p1, k1] twice, *k2tog, yo, k1, yo, SSK, [k1, p1] twice, k1; rep from * to last st, k1.

ROWS 2, 4, 6 AND 8: P3, *k1, p9; rep from * to last 4 sts, k1, p3.

ROWS 9, 11, 13 AND 15: K1, k2tog, yo, k1, yo, SSK, *[k1, p1] twice, k1, k2tog, yo, k1, yo, SSK; rep from * to last st, k1.

ROWS 10, 12, 14 AND 16: P8, *k1, p9; rep from * to last 9 sts, k1, p8.

Rep Rows 1–16.

PURSE

Cast on 47 sts. Work in St st for 1" (3cm), ending with a RS row. Knit 1 row (turning row). Work 48 rows in lace patt (3 vertical patt rep). Purl 1 row (turning row). Work in St st for 1" (3cm). Bind off.

FINISHED MEASUREMENTS

7" x 16" (18cm x 41cm), excluding purse frame

YARN

1 hank (150 yds [135m]) Kollage Illumination (mohair/viscose/polyamide blend)
> **COLOR HAZELNUT**

NEEDLES

size US 11 (8mm) straight needles

NOTIONS

sewing needle and thread

sewing machine

1 piece 17" × 16" (43cm × 41cm) fabric for lining

1 pair plastic purse handles from Sunbelt Fastener

1 yd (1m) leather cord

GAUGE

11 sts and 13½ rows = 4" (10cm) in lace patt

FINISHING

Fold the knitted piece in half longways with WS together. Seam the sides. Fold the lining fabric in half longways with WS together. With a sewing machine, seam the sides using a ½" (1cm) seam allowance. Fold the top 1" (3cm) of lining to the inside and press it flat. Place the lining inside the knit piece. Fold the knit piece to the inside at the turning row, with the top of the lining under the fold, and seam it, making sure the sts catch the outside knit fabric of the purse. Attach the handles to the top of the purse body with leather cord, making sure the cord catches inside and outside the fabric of the purse, as well as catches the lining.

NOTES

YO (YARN OVER): Wrap the working yarn around the needle clockwise and knit the next st as usual. This operation creates an eyelet hole in the knitting and inc 1 st.

K2TOG (KNIT 2 TOGETHER): Dec 1 st by knitting 2 sts tog.

NET STITCH

Work net st over a multiple of 2 sts.

ROW 1 (RS): K1 *yo, k2tog; rep from * to last st, k1.

ROW 2: Knit.

Rep Rows 1–2.

PURSE

Cast on 70 sts. Work in net st until piece measures 13" (33cm), ending with a WS row. Bind off. Weave in ends.

FINISHING

Fold the velvet fabric in half lengthwise with the long edges together and the velvet side facing out. Seam the sides, leaving 2" (5cm) open at the top of each side. Fold the top 1" (3cm) to the inside and seam the long edges to make a casing at the top edges. Insert the purse frame into the casing and assemble it by inserting the pegs from the purse frame into each end. Seam the remainder of the sides, hiding the metal purse frame.

Fold the knitted piece in half with the long edges together. Seam the sides. Stitch the knitted fabric to the velvet, just under the purse frame.

NETTED
CLUTCH

A play on the traditional springtime straw or wicker handbag, this clutch requires minimal knitting and minimal sewing...but it provides a great big impact! This bag is knit using the simplest-ever lace pattern that's stitched to a backing of black velvet. It's then sewn to a simple purse frame, and that's it! The company that manufactures the purse frames offers them in several sizes, so you can easily make a few different versions of this bag.

FINISHED MEASUREMENTS

7" × 18" (18cm × 46cm), including purse frame

YARN

1 ball (141 yds [127m]) Karabella Yarns Glimmer (rayon/lurex)
    COLOR 695 GOLD

NEEDLES

size US 8 (5mm) straight needles

If necessary, change needle size to obtain correct gauge.

NOTIONS

darning needle

sewing needle and black sewing thread

1 piece black velvet, 18" × 16" (46cm × 41cm)

16" (41cm) internal purse frame from Sunbelt Fastener (item # SFPF-IF01)

GAUGE

12 sts and 20 rows = 4" (10cm) in net st

ABBREVIATIONS

beg	BEGINNING
C5F	CABLE 5 FRONT
CC	CONTRAST COLOR
cn	CABLE NEEDLE
dec	DECREASE
dpn(s)	DOUBLE-POINTED NEEDLE(S)
foll	FOLLOWING
inc	INCREASE
k	KNIT
KFB	KNIT 1 FRONT AND BACK
k2tog	KNIT 2 TOGETHER
k3tog	KNIT 3 TOGETHER
LLI	LEFT LIFTED INCREASE
M1	MAKE ONE
MC	MAIN COLOR
p	PURL
(in) patt	(IN) PATTERN
pm	PLACE MARKER
p2tog	PURL 2 TOGETHER
p3tog	PURL 3 TOGETHER
psso	PASS SLIPPED STITCH OVER
rem	REMAINING
rep	REPEAT
RLI	RIGHT LIFTED INCREASE
RS	RIGHT SIDE
SKP	SLIP 1, KNIT 1, PASS SLIPPED STITCH OVER
SK2P	SLIP 1, KNIT 2 TOG, PASS SLIPPED STITCH OVER
sl	SLIP
SSK	SLIP, SLIP, KNIT
st(s)	STITCH(ES)
work 2 tog	WORK 2 TOGETHER
WS	WRONG SIDE
w&t	WRAP AND TURN
wyib	WITH YARN IN BACK
wyif	WITH YARN IN FRONT
yo	YARN OVER

KNITTING NEEDLE CONVERSIONS

DIAMETER (MM)	US SIZE	SUGGESTED YARN WEIGHT
2	0	LACE WEIGHT
2.25	1	LACE AND FINGERING WEIGHT
2.75	2	LACE AND FINGERING WEIGHT
3.25	3	FINGERING AND SPORT WEIGHT
3.5	4	FINGERING AND SPORT WEIGHT
3.75	5	DK AND SPORT WEIGHT
4	6	DK, SPORT AND ARAN/WORSTED WEIGHT
4.5	7	ARAN/WORSTED WEIGHT
5	8	ARAN/WORSTED AND HEAVY WORSTED WEIGHT
5.5	9	ARAN/WORSTED, HEAVY WORSTED AND CHUNKY/BULKY
6	10	CHUNKY/BULKY
6.5	10½	CHUNKY/BULKY AND SUPER BULKY
8	11	CHUNKY/BULKY AND SUPER BULKY
9	13	SUPER BULKY
10	15	SUPER BULKY
12.75	17	SUPER BULKY
15	19	SUPER BULKY
20	36	SUPER BULKY

YARN WEIGHT GUIDELINES

Because the names given to different weights of yarn can vary widely depending on the country of origin or the yarn manufacturer's preference, the Craft Yarn Council of America has put together a standard yarn weight system to impose a bit of order on the sometimes unruly yarn labels. Look for a picture of a skein of yarn with a number 1–6 on most kinds of yarn to figure out its "official" weight. Gauge is given over Stockinette stitch. The information in the chart below is taken from www.yarnstandards.com.

	SUPER BULKY (6)	BULKY (5)	MEDIUM (4)	LIGHT (3)	FINE (2)	SUPERFINE (1)
TYPE	bulky, roving	chunky, craft, rug	worsted, afghan, aran	dk, light, worsted	sport, baby	sock, fingering, baby
KNIT GAUGE RANGE	6–11 sts	12–15 sts	16–20 sts	21–24 sts	23–26 sts	27–32 sts
RECOMMENDED NEEDLE IN U.S. SIZE RANGE	11 and larger	9 to 11	7 to 9	5 to 7	3 to 5	1 to 3

SUBSTITUTING YARNS

If you substitute yarn, be sure to select a yarn of the same weight as the yarn recommended for the project. Even after checking that the recommended gauge on the yarn you plan to substitute is the same as the yarn listed in the pattern, make sure to knit a swatch to ensure the yarn and needles you are using will produce the correct gauge.

SEAMING

Many of the patterns in this book are knitted in the round to avoid seams. Generally, however, at least a small section (or sections) of the garment does need to be seamed together. You may choose any method of seaming that works best for you or with which you are familiar. Some of the best ways to seam include mattress stitch and Kitchener stitch. See page 140 of the Special Techniques Glossary for detailed instructions on mattress and Kitchener stitches.

WEAVING IN ENDS

Once your knitted piece is fully seamed together, turn it inside out and use a crochet hook or a darning needle to weave the ends in for a clean, secure finish. A crochet hook works well for weaving in short ends. If you plan to use a darning needle, make sure to leave long enough tails to easily thread through the needle. Cut off each yarn tail close to the last stitch it is woven under.

BLOCKING

Blocking can really improve the look of your finished piece. If your stitches are uneven or your knitting looks rumpled, blocking smoothes out the stitchwork. Knitted lace benefits from blocking because it opens up the delicate stitches. Blocking pieces before seaming them together can sometimes make finishing easier. If your project looks even and smooth before blocking, you can probably skip this step because it won't affect the look of your finished piece very much.

To block knitting, pin it flat—with blocking pins—to folded towels or a blocking board and then spray it with water. Allow the pieces to dry fully before removing the pins. (It is important not to pin your knitting too taut, or the sides of the knitting will pull in as it dries.) I don't recommend using an iron to block, because the heat and pressure can flatten stitches and compromise the texture and hand of natural fibers. For a quick fix, you can hold a steam iron several inches above the pinned-out pieces and steam them gently. Do not let the iron touch the surface of the knitting. Steaming can relax and even out the stitches, but it doesn't usually work quite as well as blocking.

CARING FOR YOUR KNITS

CLEANING

Wash handknits in cool water using a gentle detergent. Rinse well. Never twist or wring your knits, as this will stretch the yarns and can make it difficult to reshape the garments. Rather, squeeze out as much water as you can and then roll the knits into an absorbent towel. Then stand on the towel to remove as much water as the towel can absorb. Repeat this step using dry towels until no more water seeps to the outside of the towel. Always lay handknit garments flat to dry.

Read yarn labels carefully for care instructions, especially when using luxury yarns.

STORING

Store your handknits folded in a clean, dry place. When storing woolens, make sure to keep them away from moths. Cedar chips and lavender sachets help repel moths. Keeping garments in plastic zipper bags or airtight containers also keeps knits safe from moths. Never hang your handknits.

SPECIAL TECHNIQUES GLOSSARY

In this glossary, you'll find detailed information for all the special techniques used in the patterns collected in this book. The techniques are arranged in alphabetical order, with subentries under some of the main headings.

CASTING ON

Casting on refers to creating the number of stitches needed for the first row of any project. There are several methods for casting on. In most cases, you may use the method with which you're most comfortable. However, when a specific cast on is indicated in the pattern, it's best to follow that method because it's been used for a good reason.

BACKWARD-LOOP CAST ON

This simple cast-on method is often used to add stitches in the middle of a knitted piece as opposed to casting on stitches for the very beginning of a piece. (For example, you might use this method to cast on stitches for a buttonhole.) To cast on with the backward-loop method, simply use your fingers to make a loop in the working yarn, making sure the yarn crosses the base of the loop on the left. Slip this loop onto the needle and pull it snug. Repeat to cast on the number of stitches as indicated.

LONG-TAIL CAST ON

Leaving a long tail (approximately ½" to 1" [1cm to 3cm] for each stitch to be cast on), make a slipknot and slide it onto the right needle so the tail falls in front of the needle and the working yarn falls behind it. Insert your thumb and index finger between the yarn ends so the working yarn is around your index finger and the tail end is around your thumb. Maintain tension on the triangle you created by holding the ends with your other fingers. Turn your palm upward to make a "v" with the yarn. *Bring the needle in front of the loop on your thumb, grabbing it with the needle. Bring the needle over the strand around your index finger, pulling the resulting stitch through the loop on your thumb. Drop the loop off your thumb and, placing your thumb back into the "v" configuration, tighten the resulting stitch on the needle. Repeat from * for the number of stitches indicated.

KNITTING ON

This simple cast on is performed almost the same way as regular knitting. It uses two needles. To cast on by knitting on, make a slipknot and slide it onto the left-hand needle. Slip the right-hand needle into the loop knitwise and knit the stitch, but do not slip the loop off the left needle. Instead, transfer the new stitch from the right needle to the left. Repeat to cast on the number of stitches as indicated.

CABLES

Cabling is a technique used to cross one group of stitches in front of another. Cables are created by slipping a prescribed number of stitches onto a cable needle and holding the needle to the front or the back of the work and then knitting a certain number of stitches from the left needle. The held stitches are then knitted from the cable needle, and the row continues as usual. The number in the abbreviation is the total number of stitches involved in the cable. Divide the number in half to know how many stitches to slip to the cable needle and how many to knit from the left needle. For example, follow instructions to "C4F" (cable four front) by slipping two stitches to a cable needle and holding them in front of the work; then knit two stitches from the left needle. Finish the cable by knitting the two held stitches from the cable needle. This creates a four-stich cable that crosses to the left.

I-CORD

To make I-cord, cast on a small number of stitches—three or four works best—to one DPN. Knit one row. Slide the stitches to the opposite end of the needle. *Pulling yarn across back, knit one row. Slide the stitches to the opposite end of the needle. Repeat from * , creating I-cord. When you reach the desired length, break the yarn, pulling it tight through all the stitches. Weave the end of the yarn back through the tube. Sew the end of the I-cord to an earflap or mitten cuff to make a handy tie. Or graft the I-cord to a piece of knitted fabric with mattress stitch as a decorative element.

PAIRED DECREASES

Practically speaking, decreases reduce the number of stitches on the needles. They can also be integrated into the design when worked symmetrically, row after row, to create darts or visible lines of any other type.

KNIT TWO TOGETHER (K2TOG)

This decrease is the simplest of all. To create a right-leaning decrease, slip the right-hand needle through the first two stitches on the left-hand needle from front to back, as for a regular knit stitch. Knit the two stitches as one. To knit three together (k3tog), perform the same operation with three stitches instead of two.

SLIP, SLIP, KNIT (SSK)

This decrease slants to the left. Slip the first stitch as if to knit, slip the second stitch as if to knit, and then insert the left needle into the fronts of both stitches and knit them together.

SLIP ONE, KNIT ONE (SKP)

This is another left-slanting decrease. Slip one stitch knitwise, knit the next stitch, and then pass the slipped stitch over the knit stitch and off the needle (as when binding off).

SLIP ONE, KNIT TWO TOGETHER, PASS SLIPPED STITCH OVER (SK2P)

This is the double-decrease version of slip one, knit one (SKP). To perform this decrease, slip the first stitch knitwise, knit the next two stitches together, and then pass the slipped stitch off over the knit stitch (as when binding off).

PAIRED INCREASES

Some increases lean to the right, and others to the left. When increases are spread out evenly over several rows, it doesn't really matter which way they slant. However, increases aligned row after row are quite noticeable and become attractive design elements. Following are some of the most commonly paired increases.

LIFTED INCREASES (RLI AND LLI)

When aligned vertically, lifted increases create a defined line that makes it appear as though the increase was made a row below where it was actually created. Right- and left-lifted increases are paired to create strong lines for shaping garments.

LEFT-LIFTED INCREASE (LLI)

To create a left-leaning increase, use the left needle to lift the left leg below the stitch just knit onto the left needle. Knit the new stitch.

RIGHT-LIFTED INCREASE (RLI)

To create a right-leaning increase, use the right needle to lift the right leg of the stitch below the next stitch to be worked and place it on the left needle. Knit the new stitch.

MAKE ONE (M1)

This right-leaning increase is made by inserting the tip of the right needle from front to back into the bar between the next stitch and the stitch just knit. Place this loop onto the left needle and knit into the back of it.

MAKE ONE PURLWISE (M1P)

This left-leaning increase is made by inserting the tip of the right needle from back to front into the bar between the next stitch and the stitch just knit. Place this loop onto the left needle and knit into the front of it.

PICKING UP STITCHES

To pick up a stitch, insert the tip of one needle through the side of a stitch from front to back. Leaving about a 3" to 4" (8cm to 10cm) tail, wrap the yarn around the needle as you would for a regular knit stitch. Bring the yarn through the stitch, creating a loop on your needle. This loop is the first picked-up stitch. Continue to pick up the number of stitches required, making sure to space them evenly.

PLACING (AND SLIPPING) A MARKER (PM AND SM)

Sometimes a pattern calls for you to place a marker (pm) and slip a marker (sl marker). Markers are generally small plastic rings that slide onto a needle and rest between stitches, marking a certain spot. If you don't have markers on hand, cut small pieces of scrap yarn in a contrasting color. Tie the scrap yarn around the needle in the indicated spot in a loose knot. Move the marker from one needle to the other when you come to it. Continue as usual. Fancier beaded markers are also available.

SEAMING

Two main methods are used to seam knitted pieces together in this book. Mattress stitch is used to seam pieces with bound-off edges together, or to seam pieces together along their sides. Kitchener stitch is used to graft two rows of live stitches together. Both methods create a seamless join from the right side and Kitchener stitch is seamless from both the front and back of the work.

KITCHENER STITCH (KITCHENER ST)

To graft with Kitchener stitch, line up both sets of live stitches on two separate needles with the tips facing the same direction. Thread a yarn needle onto the tail of the back piece. Begin by performing the following steps once: Bring the needle through the first stitch on the needle closest to you as if to purl, leaving the stitch on the needle. Then insert the needle through the first stitch on the back needle as if to knit, leaving the stitch on the needle. Now you are ready to graft. *Bring the needle through the first stitch on the front needle as if to knit, slipping the stitch off the needle. Bring the needle through the next stitch on the front needle as if to purl, leaving the stitch on the needle. Then bring the needle through the first stitch on the back needle as if to purl, sliding the stitch off the needle. Bring the needle through the next stitch on the back needle, leaving the stitch on the needle. Repeat from * until all the stitches are grafted together. Approximately every 2" (5cm), tighten up the stitches, starting at the beginning of the join. Slip the tip of the yarn needle under each leg of each Kitchener stitch and pull up gently until the tension is correct. Repeat across the entire row of grafted stitches. It may help you to say to yourself, "Knit, purl – purl, knit" as you go.

MATTRESS STITCH (MATTRESS ST)

You'll work mattress stitch differently depending on whether you are seaming vertically or horizontally. For both vertical-to-vertical and horizontal-to-horizontal seaming, you'll begin the same way. Place the the blocked pieces side by side with right sides facing. With a yarn needle and yarn, insert the needle from back to front through the lowest corner stitch of one piece and then in the lowest corner stitch of the opposite piece, pulling the yarn tight to join the two pieces.

To work vertical-to-vertical mattress stitch, work back and forth as follows: On the first piece, pull the edge stitch away from the second stitch to reveal a horizontal bar. Insert the needle under the bar and pull through. Insert the needle under the parallel bar on the opposite piece and pull through. Continue in this manner, pulling the yarn tight every few rows. Weave the end into the wrong side of the fabric.

To work horizontal-to-horizontal mattress stitch, work back and forth as follows: With bound-off stitches lined up stitch-for-stitch, insert the needle under the first stitch inside the bound-off edge to one side and pull it through; then insert the needle under the parallel stitch on the other side and pull it through. Continue in this manner, pulling the yarn tight every few rows. Weave the end into the wrong side of the fabric.

SHORT ROWS

When a pattern includes short rows, you will be working partial rows, knitting or purling only a certain number of stitches before wrapping the yarn and turning the work midway through the row. Short rows create unique effects in knitted fabric, including causing the piece to swirl in a circle or to ripple. To work short rows, you'll need to perform the following two operations.

(RS) WRAP AND TURN (W&T): On the Right Side of the work, and with yarn in front, slip one stitch from left needle to right. Move the yarn to the back, slip the stitch back to the left needle and turn work. One stitch has been wrapped.

(WS) WRAP AND TURN (W&T): On the Wrong Side of the work, and with the yarn in back, slip one stitch from left needle to right. Move the yarn to the front, slip the stitch back to the left needle and turn work. One stitch has been wrapped.

Whenever you come to a wrap, work the wrap together with the stitch it wraps. To pick up a wrap and its stitch, slide the tip of the right needle into the wrap from the front of the work and place the wrap on the left needle alongside the stitch it wraps. Knit the two loops together as one stitch.

YARN RESOURCES

Each garment in this book is designed to highlight the special qualities of the luxurious yarns with which each piece is knit. You may certainly substitute other yarns for those specified, but if you'd like to knit the garments as pictured, use the following list to locate the exact yarns listed. If you are unable to find a particular yarn, visit the manufacturer's Web site for purchasing information.

This resource list cross references the specific yarn used for any given project so you can easily match what you might have in your stash with a pattern in this book. And if you're a fiber lover who chooses yarn first and pattern second, this list will help you figure out what to do with all that glorious yarn you're dying to purchase (or maybe you've already bought it and it's waiting to be knit up).

ART YARNS

www.artyarns.com

Cashmere 2, *Romantic Bell-Sleeved Cardi* (page 52); Silk Rhapsody, *Deep U-Neck Tunic Dress* (page 66)

BERROCO

www.berroco.com

Bonsai, *Bamboo Tunic* (page 22)

BLUE SKY ALPACAS

www.blueskyalpacas.com

Alpaca Silk, *Zigzag Lace Wraparound* (page 26); Brushed Suri, *Bell-Sleeved Scoop-Neck Top* (page 34); Bulky Naturals, *Short-and-Sweet Coat* (page 116)

CASCADE YARNS

www.cascadeyarns.com

Cash Vero, *Fitted Deep-Ribbed Cardigan* (page 46) and *Lace Mini-Dress* (page 62); Lana D'Oro, *Double-Breasted Cardigan* (page 90); 220 Tweed, *Texturized Tweed Coat* (page 98); Fixation, *Fur Collar* (page 122)

FUR YARN BY PAULA LISHMAN

www.furyarn.com

Fox, *Fur Collar* (page 122)

JAGGER SPUN

www.jaggeryarn.com

Zephyr Wool-Silk, *Lacy Accent Scarf* (page 124)

KARABELLA YARNS

www.karabellayarns.com

Glimmer, *Netted Clutch* (page 132)

KOLLAGE

www.kollageyarns.com

Illumination, *Openwork Handbag* (page 130)

LORNA'S LACES

www.lornaslaces.net

Swirl Chunky, *Boho Blouse* (page 30); Angel, *Lacy Dolman* (page 78)

MALABRIGO YARN

www.malabrigoyarn.com

Gruesa, *Kimono Wrap* (page 86); Aquarella, *Trapeze Jacket* (page 94) and *Full-Length Toggle Coat* (page 110); Merino Worsted, *Puffed-Sleeve Hoodie* (page 104)

MUENCH YARNS

www.muenchyarns.com

Verikeri, *Lace Sleeves* (page 126)

NEIGHBORHOOD FIBER CO.

www.neighborhoodfiberco.com

Studio Worsted Semisolid Merino, *Textured Circle Shrug* (page 82); Penthouse Silk and Loft, *Lace Panel Tunic* (page 40)

SOUTHWEST TRADING COMPANY

www.soysilk.com

Vegas, *Gold Metallic Dress* (page 72)

TILLI TOMAS

www.tillitomas.com

Pure and Simple and Disco Lights, *Silk Cami* (page 18) and *Silk Skirt* (page 58)

INDEX

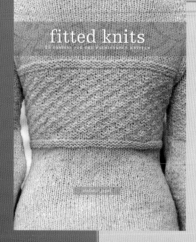
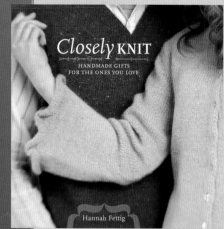
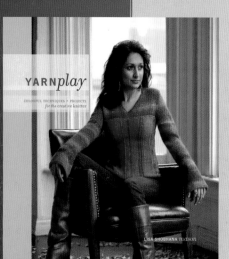